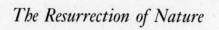

The Resurrection of Nature

The Resurrection of Nature

Political Theory and the Human Character

J. Budziszewski

Cornell University Press

Ithaca and London

First published 1986 by Cornell University Press.

International Standard Book Number 0-8014-1900-X
Library of Congress Catalog Card Number 86-6283
Printed in the United States of America
Librarians: Library of Congress cataloging information appears on the last page of the book.

The paper in this book is acid-free and meets the guidelines for permanence and durability of the Committee on Production Guidelines for Book Longevity of the Council on Library Resources.

To my grandparents,
the Reverend and Mrs. Walter B. Chrzanowski

Contents

Contents

Chapter Two
The Unity of Nature (1)
52

Chapter Three
The Unity of Nature (2)
73

Mezzalogue
The Fulfillment of Nature
95

Contents

Preface

This book makes four claims. Together, these claims supply the motive for undertaking two tasks. The claims are simply these:

1 That the last four centuries have witnessed a gradual but decisive historical retreat from the idea that Nature— *human* nature—somehow provides the rule and measure for human life.

2 That this retreat was a mistake. Not only has the abandonment of ethical naturalism greatly intensified the perplexities of moral and political life, but the arguments that have been hurled against naturalism are all invalid.

3 That despite the basic failure of the arguments against naturalism, not everything in them is wrong. All of them exploit a real vagueness in the classical concept of human nature. Some of them also uncover flaws.

4 That the classical concept of human nature can be reconstructed so as to make it both sound and precise and restore it to its original position at the center of thought on the human condition.

Thus the *tasks* of the book are, first, to achieve this reconstruction of the concept of human nature and, second, to draw its implications in morals and politics. Lazarus, come forth!

Because the book moves swiftly, an even swifter summary of

the main stages of the argument may be helpful. That argument may be broken down as follows:

Chapter One

1   The term "human nature" can be taken in three senses: that which is innate (sense one), that which is characteristic (sense two), and that which is the mark of our full and appropriate development as human beings. Confusing these three senses is a common strategy for attacking naturalism.

2   Sense three obviously gives a rule and measure for human life and social arrangements. It cannot be derived from senses one and two, although the information conveyed under these two senses may be among the circumstances relevant to its implementation.

3   That which satisfies sense three is the rational activity by which we understand ourselves and order our lives according to purposes. A great deal can be said about this ordering, despite the fact that its secular and Christian interpretations are bound to differ in very important respects.

Chapters Two and Three

4   In particular, this ordering requires that human life have a certain rational unity. Such unity applies to life as an unfolding chain of events, to the character of the agent, and to the agent's motives for action.

Mezzalogue

5   Virtues, or excellences, are those dispositions that further a life of rational unity. These excellences operate in at least four dimensions: integral, intimate, practical, and political.

Chapter Four

6   A concern for excellence requires a concern for the excellence of political institutions and policies, in the first place because individual character is deeply affected by these institutions and policies, and in the second place because

the kind of depth, commitment, and transparency that is proper to human beings requires that we share with others and that we seek with them an understanding of the common good.

7 Although contemporary liberalism is deficient in concern for the virtues, a liberal politics of virtues is not unthinkable. Whether this would be the best possible version of the politics of virtues cannot be answered at this time, although it is answerable in principle. However, because political convulsion in the name of virtue may itself be destructive to virtue, the answer to this question may be less important than one would otherwise think.

Chapter Five

8 Liberal or not, a politics of virtues also requires a theory of the proper ways in which the polity can encourage the development of the virtues among its citizens. Formal education may well be the least of these ways. Such a theory would avoid the pitfalls of past theories that followed the strategies of substitution, countervailance, sublimation, and domestication in an attempt to render virtue needless. However, it would also recognize that the demand for excellence must be moderated for the sake of excellence itself.

Preceding these chapters, the Prologue offers remarks about our current perplexity and provides an informal account of the origin of naturalism; the Epilogue had best speak for itself.

My emotional and intellectual debts to my family, friends, and colleagues are now so great that I expect them at any moment to begin proceedings for foreclosure. Perhaps I can square my debt to my wife, Sandra, by loving her in equal measure. After that I am still in the red. Following are a few pale words of thanks for all the others.

For general advice and encouragement, I thank James Austin, Bruce Buchanan, James Fishkin, Gary Freeman, H. R. Kiewiet, and Thomas K. Seung.

For very important criticism of an early prototype of the argument, I thank Douglas Rae.

Preface

For exceptionally valuable remarks on the last draft but one, I thank Brian Fay and John S. Nelson, who reviewed the manuscript for Cornell University Press.

For his support and assistance through many arduous stages of this process, I thank my editor, John G. Ackerman.

Finally, for old graces and blessings that I have never had a proper opportunity to acknowledge, I thank T. Wayne Bailey, Albert Clubock, Betty Griffin, Christopher Kelley, Keith Legg, Thomas Pangle, and, again, Douglas Rae.

J. Budziszewski

Austin, Texas

The Resurrection of Nature

The Burial of Nature

The Prologue introduces the concept of human nature as the subject of this book. Although it was at the very center of ancient reflections on morals and politics, we have inherited nothing more than a cliché. The concept must be recovered and reconstructed.

Nature as a Cliché

This age is often called skeptical. If that means that the credulity of the past has been left behind, then surely it is naive, for skepticism is the rankest kind of credulity. We do not take as verities fewer things than other ages have, but different things. One of the items in our sociological catechism is that we know more about ourselves today than at any previous time in history. The second—also taken on faith—is that moral beliefs are *never* knowledge, since they are relative to the individual, the generation, or the culture. It is almost as though we aspired to "know" everything, but to "believe" nothing. The two limbs of this paradox meet at the neck, for the third item in our catechism is that believing gets in the way of knowing. Therefore, believing nothing, like a vow of chastity, is the sacrifice that perfects our devotion to knowledge, and indifference becomes the norm of civilized conduct. Often enough we agree that we live in a moral desert, but we think the desert blooms.

How did such an arid state of affairs come to pass? I think it has to do with what might be called the life cycle of great moral ideas. Knowledge, as Bacon said, is a form of power.[1] Thus the greatest ideas are also the greatest and most constant targets of abuse—more constant even than money or rank, because everyone can gain access to an idea, but not everyone can gain access to the other two. And so the greatest ideas are always mistreated, misused, and dressed in drag until they can no longer be told from their effigies. At this point—in effigy—we burn them.

And the ideas themselves? Humiliated, but unburned after all, they take refuge in the vernacular. That is to say, they live on, but as clichés, in much the same fashion that old gods live on in superstition. The most versatile of them all happens to be very important to this book. That cliché is "human nature." It can grease the wheels of a failing argument, polish the buttons of ignorance, and evoke pride or shame at the will of the orator. Why is there war? "Human nature." Why were you unfaithful to your wife? "Human nature." Why do we do anything? "Human nature." There is no easier explanation, no easier excuse. The dons of the philosophical establishment dismiss this cliché with a snide wave of hand, and English professors warn of it in the same stern tone as sergeants warning their recruits about venereal disease; but dons and professors notwithstanding, it still makes as good a con as ever it did.

Case in point: "sociobiology." Ethology is a serious biological discipline devoted to the comparative study of animal behavior—nonhuman, and sometimes human—with an eye to its adaptive significance and to the ways in which it might have evolved through natural selection.[2] Sociobiology is an ethological fringe that has successfully passed itself off among general readers and some social scientists as its very center, if not its cutting edge. Its methods and assumptions have been widely and justly criticized. Spokesman E. O. Wilson treats complex, diverse, learned human behaviors as simple and invariant patterns for each of which there is "a gene"—for conformity, for altruism, for being a criminal, for believing in God, and in fact for so many things that one wonders whether there might also be a gene for oversimplification.[3] Compounding this is a tendency among sociobiologists to transmute "is" statements into "ought" statements in just such a way as to rationalize many of our most egregious prejudices, especially in the areas of race and class.[4] What accounts for the widespread interest in this fad?

That sociobiology cloaks our clichés in the ill-gotten garments of Science could easily be taken as the *only* reason, but I believe that there is more to it than that. Movements like this fill a void left by the great historical retreat of social scientists and students of the humanities from the concept of Nature—and this time I mean not the cliché, but the legendary ancestor of the cliché.

The Original Concept of Nature

Water is so completely the element of fish that they do not know that they are wet. Probably the earliest humans did not know that they were natural, either. The first known word for Nature belongs to the language of the ancient Greeks. Since its root was a verb meaning "to grow,"[5] that its first recorded use describes an attribute of a growing thing comes as no surprise. This use is in the Odyssey of Homer: after Odysseus and his men get into trouble with the sorceress Circe, the god Hermes offers help by showing Odysseus the powers and "nature" of a certain plant. Apparently to ask the Nature of something was to ask what were the principles by which its powers grew and came to manifest themselves. If Circe's sorcery was natural, it might have been some sort of herbal pharmacology to which Odysseus needed the antidote.

This was not an auspicious beginning, and indeed the Greeks seem to have gone on for some centuries after the era of Homer, talking about the Nature of this and that particular thing, before it dawned on a few men that all of these individual Natures might have their place in Nature-at-large, an ordered and all-embracing whole that they called a "cosmos." Now if this is true, then it must be possible to give natural explanations of everything there is, and these men—the "natural philosophers"—set out to do just that. For instance, they tried to understand the sun in terms of the properties of fiery bodies rather than in terms of the attributes of the sun god Helios.

This was a deep shock to respectable opinion. The gods were supposed to be the highest things there were. However, the finite and quarrelsome gods of myth would have to be reckoned inferior to the principles of any all-embracing Nature, and a God superior to Nature itself would give the lie to myth. Just how much of this the ordinary Greek gentleman grasped is impossible to say, but we know that he regarded the natural philosophers as atheists, or as inventors of "new gods."[6]

An even deeper shock was waiting in the wings. Theological deviants who kept to themselves could have been ignored, but the natural philosophers insisted upon applying the concept of Nature to the communities in which they lived themselves—to do to the cities what they had done to the gods. Now as every Greek knew, different cities lived differently. That was quite all right in the days before natural philosophy, when each citizen could take the way of life of his city for granted. But in order to apply the concept of Nature to the community, it was for the first time necessary to contrast Nature with Custom—in other words to contrast the principles of the full and appropriate development of human powers, with the development that human powers merely happened to achieve under the customary ways of life in the cities. Manifestly the "natural" man sought his own good. Custom demanded restraint. It followed that Custom was *un*-natural and, in particular, that there was no support in the human design for customary notions of moderation and justice. So long as he could get away with it, the natural man would seek his good without consideration for Custom. To *help* him get away with it, he would learn to *use* Custom: he would master the arts of deceptive persuasion for use in the political assemblies and the law courts.

In the heyday of this doctrine the cities were booming, and war had undermined the rural aristocracy. Democracy, where it existed, lacked the procedural safeguards we take for granted and came down to a free-for-all in which the political ambition of a sharp fellow who could outtalk, outmaneuver, and finally suppress his enemies had no limits. To youthful eyes, the "old education" looked anachronistic in its emphasis on gymnastic and revered poetry. But the "Sophists," a new breed of traveling teachers who mixed a little natural philosophy with a thorough training in rhetoric and other arts useful to the natural man, attracted a wide following and commanded high fees. The older generation was understandably scandalized. Aristophanes even wrote a play lambasting the Sophists as corrupters of the youth, the worst symptom of what he saw as the decay of the old order in Athens.[7]

Socrates—whom many of the Greeks, including Aristophanes, took to be just another Sophist himself—was the first to find the Sophistic Achilles' heel. In all of the clamor about the "natural man," no one had paused to ask what it *meant* for this natural man to seek his own good. Certainly the Sophists had not really broken free of Custom, because Custom teaches not one thing but two: not only *restraints* in the pursuit of the good things in life but also *opinions* about what the good things in life are. The Sophists had thrown off the first but remained in thrall to the second, so they were no nearer to a life according to Nature—human nature—than anyone else.[8]

As soon as customary *opinions* of the good as well as customary restraints on the pursuit of the good were hauled before the tribunal of Nature, it became clear that the political implications of the concept of Nature might be entirely different from what they had previously been taken to be. The earlier natural philosophers and their Sophistic hangers-on had discovered a conflict not really between natural desires and customary restraints, but only between *customary* desires and customary restraints. Plato soon began to teach that in the best political regime there would be no conflict between Nature and Custom at all. The citizens would pursue what was really good for them, and the way of life of the community would be so arranged as to give support to this pursuit. He admitted that the odds of such a community actually coming into existence were nil; still, his exercise provided a standard for criticizing real, *less* than perfect regimes and a basis for understanding their tensions.[9] Aristotle went even further than Plato with his profound observation that man is "by Nature a political animal"—an observation, one might add, that is usually misunderstood. He did not mean that we have an instinct for politics or anything of that sort. What he meant was that we cannot *thrive* except in a political context—that human beings can neither develop nor exercise their most truly human powers except through identification with the fortunes of some political community and participation in its customary life. Perhaps some beings can—"beasts and gods," he suggested—but they are not human, and he did not claim to speak for them.

From all of this it follows that even though Custom goes beyond Nature, it need not conflict with Nature—and may even be a natural necessity. If this is what Aristotle meant, then did he think that Nature and Custom are *never* in conflict? No; only that we cannot escape the conflict by escaping society. We have to deal with it where we sit.[10]

From such considerations these thinkers went on to compose a truly magisterial body of theory. It had its ups and downs. Although Socrates, as a martyr to Athenian wrath, became a figure of legend, Aristotle and Plato were both very nearly forgotten for a few centuries after their deaths. Nevertheless, in one form or another the concept of Nature became the very spine of what we now call "classical" thought on the ethical and political condition of the race. The early hostility of the authorities and the later suspicion of the "revealed" religions that succeeded paganism were all resolved; for instance, the late Roman legal code was explained in terms of the "law" of Nature, and the theological syntheses of the late Middle Ages were devoted to reconciling the law of Nature with the law of her Maker. Not until about the sixteenth century, after it had helped to civilize barbarian Europe, did the concept of Nature begin its decisive decline. In these times of rebarbarization, we would do well to consider its recovery.

CHAPTER ONE

The Resurrection of Nature

On the grounds that the concept of human nature was buried for very good reasons, not everyone will welcome its recovery. Chapter 1 enumerates the objections, then explicates the concept of human nature just sufficiently to refute every one of them.

Objections to the Concept of Nature

For the first few centuries of "modernity"—that is to say the entire postclassical period, from the sixteenth century to the present—philosophical writers dwelt on the subject of human nature quite as much as any classical writer did. Certainly the era was not launched with the intention of undermining the concept; in retrospect, though, that seems to have been its chief philosophical accomplishment. The gates of doubt were opened little by little until the concept of Nature was simply washed down the sluiceways into obscurity.

I reckon the number of these gates at eight: the Argument from *Is and Ought*, the Argument from *Silence*, the Argument from *Diversity*, the Argument from *Creativity*, the Argument from *Responsibility*, the Argument from *Wickedness*, the Argument from *Exile*, and the Argument from *Alienation*.

Although all of these arguments are mistaken, they do not err in every particular, and the classical concept of Nature is just foggy enough to make them plausible. What this gives us is what the medieval scholars would have called a "disputed question": *Does Nature provide the rule and measure for human life*, the norm to be followed and the standard to be applied? In fact, I have laid out this chapter according to the medieval procedure for resolving such questions. First, I summarize each of the eight arguments against the question. Then I reconstruct the concept of human nature in what I take to be its three proper senses. With the results of this reconstruction, I am armed to reply to each of the previously stated objections. The "disputation" moves very quickly but foreshadows themes to be developed in greated detail later.

The Argument from Is and Ought

According to the Argument from Is and Ought, ethical naturalism rests upon an elementary logical fallacy. This fallacy may infect other doctrines besides naturalistic doctrines. In his *Treatise of Human Nature*, published in 1739, David Hume gave the first general description of the fallacy:

> In every system of morality which I have hitherto met with, I have always remarked that the author proceeds for some time in the ordinary way of reasoning, and establishes the being of a god, or makes observations concerning human affairs; when all of a sudden I am surprised to find that instead of the usual copulation of propositions *is* and *is not*, I meet with no proposition that is not connected with an *ought* or *ought not*. This change is imperceptible, but is, however, of the last consequence. For as this *ought* or *ought not* expresses some new relation or affirmation, it is necessary that it should be observed and explained; and at the same time that a reason should be given for what seems altogether inconceivable, how this new relation can be a deduction from others which are entirely different from it.[1]

Hume's point is neither more nor less than this: because they are logically *dissimilar* to claims of what is, claims of what ought to be cannot be *deduced* from claims of what is. To use his own example, we could assert the premise (an ought-premise) that we ought to do what God commands, yet with no other premise than that God exists (an is-premise), we could draw no conclusions at all about what we ought to do. Now Hume himself did not accuse ethical naturalism of the like fallacy, but such an accusation can easily be put together, to wit: With no other premises than the facts of human nature—*is*-premises to the very last one—we can draw no conclusions at all about what we *ought* to do with ourselves. This sort of argument was first advanced by G. E. Moore in 1903.[2]

The Argument from Silence

One version of ethical naturalism, that advanced by the ancient Stoics, seems to escape from the Argument from Is and Ought in exactly the same way that divine command morality escapes from it. To the bare existence of God, the divine command moralist *adds* the premise that we ought to conform ourselves to His will. This is presented not as a deduction but as a first principle. Likewise, to the bare facts of human nature, the Stoic naturalists *added* the premise that we ought to do as Nature commands. This too was presented as a first principle rather than as a deduction. No violation of Hume's stricture is involved in either case.

The Argument from Silence aims to seal up this route of escape. Simply put, it is that nothing other than a person can issue commands. Certainly a personal God can be conceived as commanding; however, since Nature is not a person, it cannot speak for itself and must have someone to speak for it. But that really means that someone is claiming the bogus authority of Nature for what he really desires himself. It follows that although Nature can provide the conditions of human life, it can provide neither the rule nor the measure.

The Argument from Diversity

The Argument from Diversity is simply that we haven't got enough in common for "common human nature" to serve as the rule and measure of human life in the first place. Its most striking and characteristic expression is due to Thomas Hobbes, the celebrated author of *Leviathan*, published in 1641.[3] At first this is surprising because, unlike some later writers, Hobbes went out of his way to insist that the *forms* of human passion vary not a whit from individual to individual. About this, though, he was equally insistent: taken with respect to their *objects* rather than their forms, very few impulses are inherent in human flesh and soul, and such impulses as are inherent do not subscribe to any greater, preordained pattern. Consequently, men and women seek nothing but what they learn to seek, and they learn to seek different things because of the diversity of their endowments and experiences. There is no rule and measure for human life but Desire, and Desire is different in each and every one of us.

If this is true, then restraints on the pursuit of the objects of Desire can be tolerated only in the name of Desire itself. Hobbes, for instance, thought that ethics and politics were possible only because no one stands a chance of getting *any* of what he wants unless we can *all* find a way to keep from one another's throats in the meantime. His solution depended (1) on a universal *promise* to submit to common authority, and (2) on this authority having the *power* to enforce the promise.[4] Although the pages of *Leviathan* are far too heavy with the dread of anarchy and violent death for most contemporary tastes, his fundamental outlook continues to survive in utilitarianism, in "neutralism," and in many other liberal theories of politics and ethics, all characterized by the steadfast refusal to acknowledge any species of Desire as superior to any other, whether in the name of Nature or in the name of anything else.[5]

The Argument from Creativity

Although the Argument from Creativity bears some resemblance to the previous argument in its stress on human diversity, it hangs from different premises. These premises have often been given paradoxical formulations—for instance, that man is the animal "whose Nature it is to have no Nature" or "whose existence precedes his essence." More simply, the argument is that human beings must *create* whatever is to serve as the rule and measure of their lives. The only unambiguous contribution of Nature to this end is the creative impulse itself. With that exception, Nature is regarded as merely the medium in which the human artist works—at that, as a resistant medium to which he may well have to take a hammer, for like Michelangelo he thinks of his task as "liberating the figure from the marble that imprisons it." As Nietzsche cried in 1882, "one thing is needful":

> To "give style" to one's character—a great and rare art! It is practiced by those who survey the strengths and weaknesses in their nature and then fit them into an artistic plan until every one of them appears as art and reason and even weaknesses delight the eye. Here a large mass of second nature has been added; there a piece of original nature has been removed—both times through long practice and daily work at it. Here the ugly that could not be removed is concealed; there it has been reinterpreted and made sublime. Much that is vague and resisted shaping has been saved and exploited for distant views; it is meant to beckon toward the far and immeasurable. In the end, when the work is finished, it becomes evident how the constraint of a single taste governed and formed everything large and small. Whether this taste was good or bad is less important than one might suppose, if only it was a single taste![6]

Creativity in this sense is just the opposite of "letting go," for as Nietzsche says, every artist is subject to a "thousandfold laws . . . laws that precisely on account of their hardness defy all formulation through concepts."[7] And while inspired submission to these laws may be called an artist of character's "most natural" state, here the phrase is used in a self-undermining way, for the *only* "natural" impulse this state consummates is the one that aims to "conquer," "command," and "overcome" the *rest* of Nature. Or as Nietzsche liked to say even better, to "stylize" it, for the thousandfold laws that command the artist are according to him nothing more nor less than the "constraint of style."

The Argument from Responsibility

The Argument from Responsibility is simply that to act "naturally" is to act irresponsibly. For responsible action is action I take for *reasons* that I can justify to myself and to others in precisely the same way. But in the Modern understanding, Nature is a system of inherent compulsions—that is to say, not of reasons but of causes. Now either these compulsions are irresistible, or they can be resisted. If they are irresistible, then in all cases whatsoever, what I take to be my reasons for my actions are really only rationalizations for them. I already do act naturally, and the question of whether I should continue to do so is moot, because I *cannot* act responsibly. On the other hand, if these compulsions can be resisted, then in all cases where they come in conflict with reasons that I can justify to myself and to others in precisely the same way, they should indeed be resisted; but in all cases where they *coincide* with reasons that I can justify to myself and to others in precisely the same way, they are irrelevant to the justification of these reasons.

This argument owes a great deal to Immanuel Kant. Writing at the end of the eighteenth century, Kant argued that each of us should always take just those actions the underlying principles of which he can will to be laws binding upon everyone. To be responsible in this way is to be in some sense "self-legislating." To act on any other basis is to be in some sense a slave.[8]

The Argument from Wickedness

The Argument from Wickedness is that Nature cannot *provide* rule or measure for human life, because, being evil, it lacks these qualities in itself. According to Machiavelli, man's Nature is to be insatiable for gain and glory, literally "incapable of setting limits to his own fortunes." "For one can generally say this about men," he wrote around 1513,

> that they are ungrateful, fickle, simulators and deceivers, avoiders of danger, greedy for gain; and while you work for their good they are completely yours, offering you their blood, their property, their lives, and their sons . . . when danger is far away; but when it comes nearer to you they turn away. . . . And men are less hesitant about harming someone who makes himself loved than one who makes himself feared because love is held together by a chain of obligation which, since men are a sorry lot, is broken on every occasion in which their self-interest is concerned; but fear is held together by a dread of punishment which will never abandon you.[9]

Although Hobbes maintained the Arguments from Wickedness and from Diversity together in the same theory, they are logically independent; for instance, Machiavelli thought that all men, through all history, have wanted pretty much the same things, so that men are monotonous even in their fickleness.

If Nature is monotonous rather than diverse, then the fact that in its wickedness it cannot provide a rule or measure for human life does *not* imply that it cannot provide *other* useful lessons to one who can provide his *own* rule and measure; indeed, what can be more useful to the ruler of a state than a cunning familiarity with the vices that nestle in the heart of man? This cunning, blended with audacity, is precisely what Machiavelli calls the "virtue" of the ruler. Thus virtue depends on the knowledge of Nature but has no foundation in Nature itself.

The Argument from Exile

The Argument from Exile takes two forms, one of which is based on religious considerations, while the other is entirely secular. In both forms the argument is simply that somehow, during the cavernous aeons of the past, the human race compromised its own Nature. In its primal purity that Nature might truly have provided a rule and measure for human life but not in its corruption, and it is easier for a fresh carcass to rot than for a rotten carcass to freshen. The corruption will not be undone. The stain is indelible. Contemporary humanity can no more follow the Nature of its nativity than revoke its very history on second thoughts. We are in exile from the True Country and must adopt the way of life that is appropriate to exiles.

In its religious form, the Argument from Exile takes its lead from a particular (and controversial) interpretation of the allegory of the Fall in the second and third chapters of the Book of Genesis. In its outlines, the story is known to nearly everyone. God had created the first human beings happy and whole but with liberty to fall from their perfection by disobedience; otherwise, they would have been his pets rather than his friends. The object of their eventual disobedience was a tree in the very heart of their garden domain, whose fruit God had forbidden them to eat. They made this fruit their object by the misdirection of three otherwise good impulses, which are given in Genesis as pleasure in the satisfaction of appetite, pleasure in beauty, and the desire for wisdom.[10] This misdirection was prompted by the idea of becoming "like gods"; since the tree is called the "tree of knowledge of good and evil," this probably means appropriating the Divine prerogative of setting moral values on things. It seemed to be a reasonable project because they had already allowed themselves to be convinced that God had deceived them. His deceit was to claim that eating the fruit of the tree would bring death. But this was *not* a deceit, for it did bring death—according to this interpretation of the story, death in three senses. First, expulsion from their first home made the bodies of these first humans liable to return (after a span of years) to dust; we may call this physical death. Second, disobedience had isolated them from God, in Whom alone they could know themselves; we may call this spiritual death. Third, the *manner* of their disobedience laid the pattern, in perpetuity, for errancy in the impulses that were originally given by God; although the book of Genesis has no word for Nature at all, under the terms of this interpretation we may call this natural death. Obviously, errant impulses cannot provide a reliable rule and measure for human life. Thus threefold death brought pain, sorrow, and labor into the world, and—on some interpretations—property, despotism, and the distinction of ranks as well.

The argument concludes that human beings *can* be redeemed from death in this life but only by Grace, which is God's side of a supernatural covenant in which the soul surrenders her Will and her Nature to their Author. Since God covenants Grace only with individuals, since He administers the covenant Himself, and since it is beyond codification, by the terms of this interpretation no heartening implications follow for the conduct of unredeemed public life. Moral and political philosophy presuppose, and must presuppose, dead Nature rather than redeemed Nature.[11] In the end, the political implications of this argument are very like those of the Argument from Wickedness.

In its *second* form, despite an apparently secular basis, the Argument from Exile continues to echo the themes of Fall, Sorrow, and Redemption. In the hands of some writers it presents a romantic face that contemplates redemption as personal; in the hands of others it presents a civic face that contemplates redemption as political. In fact, the two faces are not far distant and sometimes gaze into each other's eyes, but only the second concerns us here.

A special feature of secular redemption is that the thing that is redeemed usually turns out to be a simulacrum of the Nature that was lost rather than the genuine article. Jean-Jacques Rousseau, for instance, conceived a pilgrimage from "natural" freedom and equality, through various epochs of despotism and inequality, to "civic" freedom and equality; but since the human race of one age is not the human race of another, the two kinds of freedom, no less the two kinds of equality, are alike only in externals. Primal or natural man was free in that he followed no law but that of his own will, and equal because—having few needs—he was independent of every other man. By contrast, social man is free if and when he recognizes his will *in* the law of his republic, and equal if and when the dependence of every individual upon every other is so *complete* that their civic wills are as though one.[12] Likewise, Karl Marx conceived a pilgrimage from "primitive" or natural communism, through various epochs of alienation, to "true" communism; but true communism bears only a superficial resemblance to primitive communism because the former was under the law of natural necessity while the latter is under the law of "freedom."[13]

The Argument from Alienation

In several points, the Argument from Alienation merely recapitulates the Argument from Exile in its secular form; it agrees that man is somehow at odds with his own Nature and that progressive alienation from his Nature is what history is all about. But it sharply departs from the Argument from Exile in regarding this alienation as a *good* thing rather than a corruption. Hence, redemption is something most earnestly to be avoided. Man becomes *human* in this view, becomes "Man properly so-called," *precisely* by setting himself at odds with his own Nature, and for that matter with anything else that presents itself as merely "given." He becomes human, in other words, at the same moment that he escapes from Nature into "history." Should history ever come to an end—that is to say, should humans ever cease to be at odds with their own Nature and every other "given"—then they would cease to be human and become animals again, albeit animals whose continuing mastery of technology guaranteed them plenty of everything. To say that

Nature should provide the rule and measure of human life, therefore, is as much as to say that man should abdicate his specifically human character.

Alexandre Kojève makes this point by way of an interpretation of Hegel and Marx which is more radical than the one I presuppose in my remarks on the secular form of the Argument from Exile; however, the interest in Kojève's point is independent of the truth of his interpretation of Hegel and Marx, and his remarks are worth quoting at some length. The following passage is from the first edition of his *Introduction to the Reading of Hegel* (1946):

> The disappearance of Man at the end of History, therefore, is not a cosmic catastrophe; the natural World remains what it has been from all eternity. And therefore, it is not a biological catastrophe either: Man remains alive as animal in *harmony* with Nature or given Being. What disappears is Man properly so-called—that is, Action negating the given. . . . Practically this means: the disappearance of wars and bloody revolutions. And also the disappearance of Philosophy. . . . But all the rest can be preserved indifinitely; art, love, play, etc., etc.; in short, everything that makes man *happy*.

Perhaps this does not sound so bad. But to the text of his second edition, Kojève added second thoughts:

> The text of the preceding note is ambiguous, not to say contradictory. . . . If Man becomes an animal again, his arts, his loves, and his play must also become purely "natural" again. Hence it would have to be admitted that after the end of History, men would construct their edifices and works of art as birds build their nests and spiders build their webs, would perform musical concerts after the fashion of frogs and cicadas, would play like young animals, and would indulge in love like young beasts. . . . Animals of the species *Homo sapiens* would react by conditioned reflexes to vocal signals or sign "language," and thus their so-called "discourses" would be like what is supposed to be the "language" of bees. What would disappear, then, is not only Philosophy or the search for discursive Wisdom, but also that Wisdom itself.[14]

Scholars being what they are, after these second thoughts Kojève went on to entertain *third* thoughts about the end of history, but since these have no bearing on his horror over the prospect of man's reintegration with Nature, they do not concern us here.

The Arguments against Nature are now complete.

Reconstruction of the Concept of Nature

What *is* human nature? My youngest daughter asks a lot of questions, but she is still learning the meanings of words. If she were to ask me, "Daddy, what's my weight?" I might be uncertain whether she wanted a *definition* or a *description*. In the first case she would be asking what "weight" or "my weight" means in general; I might reply, "Weight is what makes you hard to pick up. If you weigh a lot, you're very hard to pick up, but if you weigh only a little, then you're not very hard to pick up." On the other hand, she might already know that and simply want to know her own weight. In this case I might say something like, "Well, you weigh so-and-so-many pounds. That means you weigh a lot more than that great big doll over there, but not as much as your sister here," and dramatize by picking up each in turn with various amounts of huffing and puffing. If I misconstrued her question and started huffing and puffing and picking things up before she knew what "weight" means in general, I would probably only confuse her; if I gave her a definition of weight when she really wanted me to size her up against her doll and her sister, I wouldn't do any better.

With children, mistakes like this are usually harmless. Children are used to being misunderstood by adults, and if not eloquent, they are at least persistent enough to keep asking questions until they find out what they want to know. By contrast, adults are misled by their own command of language. They are so quick to assume that they understand each other that they often fail to find out whether they really do. If someone asks me what human nature is, I may assume that he wants a definition, and give him one. Then again he may just want a description. Since the term "human nature" is used in several distinct but related senses, he may have in mind a different sense than I have;

33

in this case he may fail to recognize my definition and think that I *am* giving him a description. No doubt he will find my "description" a poor one, and rather than asking a follow-up question, he will go away unsatisfied.

The multiplicity of meanings for the term "human nature" is not a particularly modern problem, but it has been such a long time since most philosophers have thought hard on Nature that we are less aware of the problem than we used to be. Consider the medieval Aristotelians: a prejudice left over from their defeat at the dawn of the modern era is that they were a pack of hair-splitters. Some of these hairs we might ourselves do well to split now and then. They typically distinguished between that which is "given by Nature," that to which we are "inclined by Nature," and that which is necessary for the "perfection" of Nature; alternatively, between Nature in the sense of impulses to action that are inherent to mortal flesh, Nature in the sense of patterns of action that are followed by the great majority of human beings in almost all times and places, and Nature in the sense of principles of action that mature reason recognizes as necessary to make us good instances of our kind. What held these three senses together was the belief that God had placed the same impulses in the flesh of everyone, that He had done so according to particular purposes, and that our reason has been given us to understand these purposes and to align ourselves with them.

What happened at the very end of the Middle Ages and in the first part of the modern era is that a few threads were plucked from this belief so that the three senses of Nature began to ravel away from one another. In the following centuries few have thought of weaving them back into the same tapestry. Needless to say—or is it needless?—this sharply curtails the moral uses to which the concept of Nature can be put. We need a richer loom. One color is not enough to weave the human tapestry in all its natural hues.

I don't know whether I can weave such tapestries myself, but I can try to prepare the loom. The primary colors seem to me to be three: Nature in the sense of the innate; Nature in the sense of the characteristic; and Nature in the sense of the full and appropriate. The medieval followers of Aristotle had the right idea, but their colors were not pure and their eye was not true: their colors were tainted by unsupportable assumptions, and their eye wandered too much from its object. We will begin again.

Nature as the Innate

"The innate" takes in whatever there is in what we do, what we think, and what we feel that we do not have to learn. There is one complication: learning *is* one of the things that we "do." Teachers like to say that we even learn to learn. However, nothing in the way we learn that must itself be learned can be called innate. The only part of the way we learn that comes under the rubric of the innate is the part that does not have to be learned.

Some seventeenth-century philosophers thought of the human soul as a blank slate upon which characters can be written only by experience. Could it be that *nothing* in us is innate? We don't know enough to say with certainty just how *much* is innate in what we do, think, and feel, but logic alone shows that *something* must be. If nothing were innate, then everything would have to be learned. If everything had to be learned, then of course everything in the way we learn would also have to be learned. But if everything in the way we learn had to be learned, then we could never begin to learn in the first place. Since we *do* learn, this cannot be correct, so something must be innate.

For instance, suppose someone were to say that we become what we are simply because of the conditioning we receive—that we tend to repeat pleasurable experiences and tend not to repeat painful experiences. Then we should have to ask what makes some experiences pleasurable and other experiences painful. If the reply were that this is predetermined by the structure of the nervous system, then we would have found something innate. If the reply were that we *learn* when to feel pleasure and when to feel pain, then we should have to return to the beginning. Clearly *this* learning would not be conditioning, so we would have to ask all over again how it works. No matter what the answer, the next question would have to be what makes it work in just that way and not in another—the same question previously asked about conditioning. Unless we permitted an infinite regress, eventually this cross-examination would show that the celebrated slate is not blank after all.

35

My own suspicion is that learning is the *only* area of doing, thinking, and feeling where we will find much that is innate. Of course, this may be wrong. On the other hand, it is certainly true that in order to begin disentangling what is innate from what is not innate (the latter category including everything that is natural in some other sense), we will have to pay a great deal of attention to the way we learn.

Nature as the Characteristic

Whatever we do, think, and feel that is not innate, we have somehow learned. Obviously we do not all learn the same things. However, because our physical constitution suits us for similar experiences, and because we learn largely from one another, and because *something* in the way we learn does not have to be learned—we do bear a certain resemblance to one another. Now things can be similar in different senses: in what they lack, or in what they have; in what they are not, or in what they are; in what they are not like, or in what they are like—briefly, in either a negative or a positive sense. A duck and a thunderstorm are similar in that neither is a meteor. A duck and an eagle are similar in that both are birds. The second kind of similarity is the kind I have in mind: we are variations on a single theme.

Let us use the adjective "typical" for all of the possibilities of doing, thinking, and feeling which, while not known before being learned, are almost certain to *be* learned—with the important proviso that just *what* is almost certain to be learned is likely to depend in part on our physical and cultural surroundings. The "passions," for instance, are typical: although rage, envy, pity, love, and shame all have to be learned, we usually do learn them. Yet it is a commonplace that their forms vary from culture to culture, and there may be some passions that are typical to some cultures but not typical to others in any form at all.[15]

Now we are not indifferent to our surroundings, nor should we be; for just as some physical surroundings are more suited than others to the health of our bodies, some cultural surroundings are more suited than others to the flourishing of our souls—and I think we could agree about this even without agreeing about what it means for our souls to flourish. Simply for the sake of definition, let us call any cultural surroundings that do not *preclude* the flourishing of our souls "natural" surroundings (and leave open the question whether we always flourish whenever nothing precludes our flourishing). This definition allows us to set aside a certain *subset* of the typical: namely, that which is typical to *natural* surroundings. The name I am going to use for this subset is the "characteristic." Thus the characteristic takes in all the possibilities of doing, thinking, and feeling which, while not known before being learned, are almost certain to *be* learned in surroundings that do not preclude our flourishing.

I note in passing that the distinction between the innate and the typical can be drawn without considering what is good for us, but that the distinction between the typical and the characteristic presupposes the knowledge of what is good for us. Thus the definition of the characteristic anticipates the definition of the full and appropriate.

Nature as the Full and Appropriate

Since the seventeenth century, whenever we have wanted to understand something, we have been likely to begin by taking it apart, as we take apart a watch to see how it ticks. Things are understood less in terms of the scheme of things to which they belong than in terms of the interaction of their elements. To be sure, the classical philosophers too were interested in the interaction among the elements of the things they studied; nevertheless, they began differently. When a classical philosopher wanted to understand something, the first thing he tended to do was try to figure out the class of things to which it belonged "by Nature." The second was to discern its differences from other things in that class. The third was to discover its *ergon*—translated sometimes as "function" but better as "proper work"—which Plato defined simply as "that which one can only do with it, or best with it."[16] Thus the class of things to which a watch belongs is the class of machines; what distinguishes it from other machines seems to be the sweep of its hands with the hours of the day; and its proper work is keeping time.

Aristotle saw no reason not to apply the same method everywhere, even to the understanding of human beings. First, he pointed out that we belong to the class of animals. Then, impressed that what distinguishes us from other animals is the possession of reason, he concluded that the *exercise* of reason is involved in our proper work. This is what led him to posit as the foundation of his ethics that what is good for us—what is in the highest sense natural for human beings, the thing wherein we come into our own, the thing wherein we flourish, the measure of our full and appropriate development, and the rule of our conduct—is "an activity of the soul which follows a rational principle."[17] The term "rational" in this expression must be understood broadly. Aristotle was not talking about deductive, technical, or narrowly instrumental reasoning, which we might call "ratiocination"; he was talking about the activity by which we understand ourselves, bring our lives into purposeful order, and keep them in this order. This, he regarded as the fitting completion of the potential that only human beings among all earthly creatures possess.

Now there are problems with this procedure for understanding human beings. In the first place, both the proper work of every individual thing and the proper way of situating it in a classification depend on the purposes of its proper user, or the one who properly directs its use. For example, for me to put a rock to work in fending off an attacker is no less proper than for me to put it to work in shimming up a leg of my wobbly table or in building a wall around my house. The rock may have many differences from other objects, but which of these differences *matter* depend upon which of these three works I have in mind. God may indeed have intended certain things for certain kinds of uses, as in Christian theology He is held to have done. However, since we cannot simply read off His purposes from the manifold physical characteristics of the objects he has placed before us, He must have intended us to discern them by some method other than Aristotle's. Otherwise, we might be like the Englishmen of another day who thought that God had intended foxes for the pleasure of the lords in hunting them. By the same token, we cannot conclude that the proper work of a human being involves the exercise of reason *simply because* no other animal possesses reason; no other animal gets red cheeks either—as Aristotle himself remarked—yet we do not say that the proper work of a human being is shame. To call attention to the lack of reason in other animals is meaningful only if we *already* recognize the exercise of reason as involved in our proper work.

Should we recognize it as such? I have reviewed the fallacies of Aristotle's procedure not because I reject his conclusions, but because the fallacies of his procedure have often before this been *thought* sufficient grounds to reject his conclusions. To my mind, instead of deriving his conclusions by means of his dubious procedure, he should have stated them as an undemonstrable first principle—more precisely, as a principle that can be vindicated, but only by mature self-examination and not by pure logic: that the good of the soul is found in the rational activity by which we understand ourselves and order our lives according to purposes. This is our "natural" good simply in this sense: in no other understanding of our full and appropriate development can souls *so constituted as we are* come to rest. They cannot rest in pleasure, honor, or any of the other candidates.

We should not need philosophers to convince us of this. In his own discussion of the candidates, even Aristotle ended by appealing to common experience. We should take Mick Jagger seriously when he sings that he "can't get no satisfaction." All the same, this may seem to be an evasion—as though I were quite willing to provide an explication but unwilling to provide an argument. On the contrary, since my object is not to give an axiomatic proof of my claim about rational purpose but to recommend it to mature self-examination, this is a case where an *adequate* explication *is* the right kind of argument. The most plausible objections to my proposition, I believe, would come from either misunderstandings about what it means or misunderstandings of what it does not mean. Concerning what it means, for instance, one might get the idea that I recommend that calculating scarecrow, *Homo oeconomicus*, as the model of the good life; or concerning what it does not mean, one might get the idea that I prohibit spontaneity or free play, or that I regard as nonsense the Christian's sense of his ultimate dependence upon God. But I can do something about suspicions like these.

Suspicions of the first kind can best be allayed in Chapters 2 and 3, where I describe the life of rational purpose and self-understanding in terms of three kinds of "rational unity": the kind the individual needs in his whole life as an unfolding chain of events, the kind he needs in his character or moral personality, and the kind he needs among his motives for action. For everything there is a season, and a time for every matter under heaven: no doubt! But whatever the time or season for the calculation of costs and benefits, I hope to make clear that this activity provides no model for the rational activity of the soul.

I can best allay suspicions of the second kind by taking them up piecemeal. One way to do this is to show that goods purported to be ultimate are really secondary and qualified. Arguments of this kind abound in Aristotle's *Ethics*. For instance in Book I, Chapter 5, he is concerned with the suspicion that honor—the preeminent concern of his cultivated and well-born readers—is better than anything else. But what he shows them is that they desire above all to be honored for qualities they really possess—in particular, for excellence of character; thus they had considered excellence of character better than honor all along, but had not known it. This strategy is also effective against the possible objection that the rational purpose thesis prohibits spontaneity and free play. On the contrary: play is delightful as a manifestation of *richness* of purpose, as an exercise of the capacities *involved* in purposeful pursuit, and as a simple rest from labor. However, if play fills the entire canvas of life, it loses its delight, becoming no longer play but dissipation. The upshot is that play should not be conceived as an alternative to purposefulness in the first place; what considerable value it has, it acquires only against a purposeful backdrop.

A slightly different strategy is needed against the Christian objection, that being to show that it is not a Christian objection at all. There is no inconsistency in saying, by the light of Nature, that our full and appropriate development is marked by rational purpose and self-understanding—and adding, by the light of Grace, that the soul must find her purposes in the will of Him who made her and only There seek the truth of herself. God is not called the Father of Lights for nothing. I owe these insights to Christian thinkers like Augustine and Thomas Aquinas, for the problem was thoroughly thrashed out during the first thirteen centuries of the Church. They would have said that Christianity does not offer an *objection* to ethical naturalism but confronts it with a *choice*, than which none can be more fateful: between Nature as seen in its own glow, and Nature as brilliantly illuminated from behind.

My own choice is unequivocally for the second kind of naturalism. Secular naturalism can provide a teleological unity to our moral reflections, and that is not to be taken lightly; but in the first place the unity it provides is incomplete because the most disturbing questions are beyond its reach, and in the second place the teleology it offers has no power to validate itself. To speak of understandings outside of which beings so constituted as we are cannot come to rest is very good, but ultimately one must ask questions about the Source of that constitution. Nevertheless, in this book my focus is on the ground that secular and Christian naturalism have in common. Besides promoting naturalism, I would like to make it possible for the two sides to talk.

To return then to my main theme—the proposition about rational purpose and self-understanding—I should mention that no matter how many suspicions I address, there are no arguments that will persuade everybody. If Norman O. Brown, for instance, should continue to sing paeans to "polymorphous perversity," one should greatly suspect that we would have nothing to say to one another.[18] This is an ineradicable inconvenience of ethics (and not only naturalistic ethics). But that is no objection at all, because it is also an ineradicable inconvenience of every field of knowledge. To the dismay of foundationalists, geometry teachers do run into students who just can't see why, on flat surfaces, parallel lines never meet. That is why the prefaces to mathematics textbooks often appeal to something called the "mathematical maturity" of the student—analogously, why Aristotle considered it a waste of time (and probably dangerous) to try to teach ethical theory to students who hadn't at least the rudiments of good character. That will not sit easily with everyone. Very well; should the inconvenience of the field be found insufferable, I will raise no objection to throwing out all the books on ethical theory, provided only that everything else in the library is thrown out too.

To conclude this section: now that the term "Nature" has been parsed into three senses—the innate, the characteristic, and the full and appropriate—what is the relation between them?

41

Four points seem important here. (1) The third sense is the one that gives a rule and measure for human life. It cannot be derived from senses one and two; however, the information conveyed under these three senses may be among the circumstances relevant to its implementation. The gratification of the passions is not the good of life, but in prescribing virtues to those who recognize the good as rational purpose and self-understanding, it certainly helps to know the passions they experience. Now, in rapid order, (2) our innate endowments are such that it is *possible* to progress in the direction of our full and appropriate development; (3) our characteristic development is such that we can be brought to see the *desirability* of such progress; but (4) our characteristic development is also such that this progress is very difficult and retrograde movement very tempting. We develop the passions and capacities called upon by virtue with relative ease. But the vices call upon the selfsame passions and capacities. Only with great effort do we learn to call upon them in the ways that do us good.

The last three points suggest that even though our characteristic development can be regarded as a kind of platform or preparation for our full and appropriate development, we are still confronted with certain powerful tensions between the two. Both secular and Christian naturalists have called attention to these tensions, although Christian naturalists have done so more emphatically. Thomas Aquinas, for instance, took the position that the "law of sin," before which St. Paul found himself helpless without the aid of Grace, is a congenital weakness of human reason with respect to the passions, which it is the office of reason to direct. He considered this a penalty for the fact that from earliest times human beings have not submitted their Nature to its Author.[19] This interpretation is hardly likely to find favor with secular naturalists. But however these tensions are accounted for, and whether or not Grace is considered necessary for their resolution, they are what makes the second problem of rational unity (the rational unity of character) such an important issue in Chapter 3.

Granted that our natural good is found in rational purpose and self-understanding, secondary truths flow from the facts that we cannot thrive equally through *all* forms of purposeful activity, and that we depend on one another for the achievement of the conditions that our thriving requires. At length, this will lead us not only back to the classical doctrine of the "virtues" but even into considerations of politics.

Replies to the Previous Objections

Our disputed question is whether Nature provides the rule and measure for human life. Eight arguments have been raised in objection.

The *Argument from Is and Ought* is that moral conclusions cannot be deduced from factual premises.

The *Argument from Silence* is that cannot do what Nature commands because Nature cannot speak for itself.

The *Argument from Diversity* is that we haven't got enough in common for "common human nature" to serve as the rule and measure for human life in the first place.

The *Argument from Creativity* is that human beings must *create* whatever is to serve as the rule and measure for their lives.

The *Argument from Responsibility* is that since Nature is a system of causes rather than a system of reasons, to act "naturally" is to act irresponsibly.

The *Argument from Wickedness* is that Nature cannot *provide* rule or measure for human life because, being evil, it lacks these qualities in itself.

The *Argument from Exile*, in both its religious and secular forms, is that although Nature might have provided a rule and measure for human life in its primal purity, it has been irremediably corrupted with the course of time.

The *Argument from Alienation* is that we owe our specifically human character to just this "corruption."

With the advantage of the preceding reconstruction of the concept of Nature, I will go ahead to show quickly where each of these eight arguments fails.

Reply to the Argument from Is and Ought

Obviously it is true that an "ought" can never be deduced from an "is," if this means that a moral fact can never be deduced

43

from a nonmoral fact. But ethical naturalism does not involve the claim that moral facts can be deduced from nonmoral facts. It involves only the claim that there *are* such things as moral facts— something even Moore admitted, although he failed to recognize their natural status. That human beings are subject to passions— this is a nonmoral fact, neither good nor bad; it figures in a great deal of moral reasoning but only in conjunction with moral facts rather than by itself. That the rule of human life is to seek the comprehensive good, that the measure of this good is the rational activity by which we understand ourselves and order our lives according to purposes—these, by contrast, are moral facts, the first moral facts, from which all others flow.

Let it be noted that agreeing with Hume that moral facts can never be deduced from nonmoral facts is not the same as accepting the "fact-value distinction." On its terms, there are no moral facts at all, for values have no objective status. Although Hume is often alleged to be the originator of this dubious distinction, it is a subjectivistic misinterpretation of what he really said.

Reply to the Argument from Silence

To this extent the Argument from Silence is correct: that whatever may be admirable in creeds like the Stoic, their epistemologies are defective. Debate over whether Nature can speak for itself confuses the issue of whether naturalism makes sense by conjuring an image of Nature as something *outside* us to which we must listen. But human nature is not something outside us; it is something *about* us. That was the reason for the wording given in the reconstruction of the third sense of the term "Nature": self-understanding and rational purpose are our "natural" good simply in this sense, that *in no other understanding of our full and appropriate development can souls so constituted as we are come to rest.*

The same point may be put in more contemporary terms. Briefly, we arrive at the truth about our full and appropriate development not by listening to the oracles of the Roman goddess Natura but in a "reflective equilibrium" conditioned by our characteristic impulses and by what we know about them. If we like, we may continue to say that Nature "speaks"—but only metaphorically.

44

Reply to the Argument from Diversity

Obviously, we do not all learn the same things; further, we may not even have *precisely* the same endowment of those innate features (whatever they are) that pattern learning. But this in no way demonstrates that Nature cannot provide the rule and measure for human life. As already shown, something can be natural to us in any of three different senses. The fundamental task of moral theory is to describe what is naturally *good* for us, and this falls not under the rubric of our innate endowments but under the rubric of their full and appropriate development.

The question, then, is not whether we are alike in everything that we want, but whether we are alike in what makes us human. To imagine a human being for whom self-understanding and rational purpose were *not* good would be difficult in the extreme. So long as discrepancies among our innate endowments and possible experiences are not so great as to imply discrepancies in the most general and fundamental conditions and principles of our flourishing—so long as it is still possible to speak *not only* of what is good for us as individuals, each with his own experiences, makeup, culture, and calling, but also (and more deeply) of what is good for us simply as human beings—we are on firm ground.

Reply to the Argument from Creativity

The crafting of a life may be an art, but it is not a nonrepresentational art; the idea is to liberate a *human* figure from the marble that imprisons it, and fidelity to that goal is more important than novelty. Nietzsche was quite right to emphasize the "thousandfold laws" to which the artist must pledge himself in order to liberate that figure. They are every bit as immutable as he claimed. But Nietzsche was only half right in identifying Nature with the marble that imprisons that figure, for the figure is also Nature: the marble is Nature in the sense of the characteristic, while the figure is Nature in the sense of the full and appropriate.

Nietzsche seems also to have seriously misunderstood the "constraint of style." One acquires style by trying to be a good human being; one does not become a good human being by

45

trying to acquire style. From this we can recognize just what these "thousandfold laws" really are. In another age they were called the Laws of Nature.

Reply to the Argument from Responsibility

The Argument from Responsibility *depends* upon a concept of human nature. Kant himself rightly regarded us as by Nature *rational*, an implication of which, he thought, is that we are also answerable to one another. Since he never claimed that we always live up to this standard, he was clearly contemplating Nature in its third sense, as our full and appropriate development. The only thing this leaves out of account is what our full and appropriate development is a development *of*. To set natural reason and the rest of Nature in separate compartments—as though either the head could be abstracted from the heart or the heart from the head—is an error; in fact, there is always some heart in every thought and some thought with every passion. Natural reason is not a substitute for the passions but their completion.

For illustration, it is quite all right to say that we best realize our rational nature when we act responsibly, and that responsible action is action according to reasons that I can justify to myself and to others in precisely the same way. But why would I *want* to be authentically justified before others, were I not so made that I cannot live meaningfully except in society? This is not something that follows from the mere fact of rationality; we can easily conceive of rational beings who are not social. It follows rather from the *kind* of rational beings we are. And we are that kind, because of the *particular* characteristic impulses of which our natural reason is the completion.

This reply may be summarized as follows. (1) Closely regarded, the Argument from Responsibility is not antagonistic to the claim that Nature provides the rule and measure for human life after all. On the contrary, (2) it rightly presupposes that the rule and measure for human life has its foundation in our rational nature. However, (3) its account of natural reason is misleading because it tries to develop this account in abstraction from the other aspects of human nature.

Reply to the Argument from Wickedness

This argument, although unable to defeat natural philosophy, does show the need for modifications to its classical form.

The first point of this reply is that the very persistence of our description of ourselves as "wicked" suggests an enduring awareness of a good that we persistently fail to achieve. Although I take this to be the same natural good that I have already described, the implication is puzzling. For Nature to provide the end without providing the means would be strange not only from a metaphysical standpoint but even from the standpoint of natural selection.

Now if human nature really did lack all means for its own regulation, then in order to keep their passions at bay, the people really would require a Prince. But for the same reason the Prince would also require a Prince; and none could be found, for his cunning would always be consumed by his intemperance. In fact, Machiavelli declares that the passions of the Prince "are much greater than those of the people." Conversely, if the cunning of the Prince is not always consumed by his intemperance, then human nature does—at least in part—possess the means for its own regulation. In places, Machiavelli admits this. But if human nature does possess means for its own regulation, then to persist in applying these means to anything but our natural good would be bizarre.

I would like to stop here, but an objection comes from the fact that we do so persist. Although I cannot explain this persistence away, at least I can reply that we are not *compelled* to persist. The response requires a momentary digression.

To ask, "What are the good things in life?" is an error. We should ask rather, "What kinds of life are good?" For the good things are not always good; they are good in *those* lives and not otherwise. Pursued as targets of opportunity or as ultimate ends, they draw a different web of life around them, a life that tangles and frustrates our deepest longings. Evil, then—that portion of evil for which we are responsible—is the placing of a partial good in the place of the comprehensive good, or the twisting of a partial good from the pattern that *makes* it good: an unraveling of threads from the tapestry.

Now the classical philosophers believed that we do evil only through ignorance of this pattern or of its correct application under particular circumstances; the second of these two kinds of ignorance, they held, is especially likely when intellect is clouded by passion. That is a plausible answer, but incomplete. We sometimes *fight* to remain ignorant, which is a defect of will, not of reason—choosing partial goods in the full knowledge that they are partial, and submitting to the gravest lacerations of spirit rather than following our deepest longings. It is no good saying that in this case the longings in question must not be our deepest. Why we persist in such choices is a mystery beyond philosophy—a matter, I think, for theology; but mysterious choices are still choices.

If we were *not* prone to such choices, natural philosophy would be unproblematic and perhaps would never have been abandoned—unless on the grounds that it was superfluous. And if we were prone to such choices but could not *recognize* them as evil, natural philosophy would deserve to have been abandoned. Good riddance. But since we *are* prone to such choices *yet recognize them as evil*, we have not only to resurrect natural philosophy but also to compel it to own up to a vocation it did not follow among the Greeks: to *draw the implications of Nature even in its frustration*. This is a problem to which I return later, especially in the fifth chapter.

Reply to the Argument from Exile

The gist of this reply is that most of its work has already been done—something that the rhetorical similarity between the religious and secular forms of the Argument from Exile obscures—for its religious form is closely related to the Argument from Wickedness, while its secular form is closely related to the Argument from Responsibility.

In its religious form, the Argument from Exile is really an allegorical realization of the Argument from Wickedness in all respects save this: that from the outset it *admits* almost all the points made in the *reply* to the argument. For instance, the Reply to the Argument from Wickedness explains the persistence of the sense of wickedness in terms of an enduring awareness of a natural good that we persistently fail to achieve; so does the religious form of the Argument from Exile. Likewise, the Reply to the Argument from Wickedness characterizes evil in terms of the substitution of partial goods for the comprehensive good; again, so does the religious form of the Argument from Exile. The only respect in which these two lines of reasoning *decisively* diverge is in the insistence of the latter that human nature has suffered "death" and in the interpretation placed on that term. Here it fails. For if human nature had really died utterly, then the awareness of a natural good that we persistently fail to achieve could not endure at all—and it does endure.

By the way, the theology offered by this argument differs from that traditionally accepted among Christians. In the traditional interpretation of the story of the Fall, human nature is not dead but mortally wounded. That is an important distinction: after all, dying men know what life is, and dead men do not. Tradition agrees that redemption and healing are not possible without the assistance of Grace but does not agree in denying the reality of human efforts at virtue. The nontraditional interpretation dates only to the Reformation, when men like Luther and Calvin decided that admitting the reality of human efforts at virtue was tantamount to admitting their sufficiency.

Now as to the secular form of the Argument from Exile, first, I would like to emphasize something that we have already seen: that in this form, the argument culminates in a distinction between natural necessity and "freedom." But this distinction is not materially different from one we have seen in the Argument from *Responsibility:* namely, between natural compulsion and "self-legislation." In fact, the only real difference between these two arguments is that while the Argument from Responsibility develops its concepts of necessity and freedom in the abstract, the Argument from Exile in its secular form finds the corresponding realities somewhere in history. Whether this is a good or bad theory of history is irrelevant for our present purposes. We need only know whether distinguishing between necessity and freedom undermines ethical naturalism, and we have seen in the fifth reply that it does not.

Reply to the Argument from Alienation

As we have just seen, the reply to the secular form of the Argument from Exile is greatly simplified by the fact that in large part it is just a historical realization of another argument. Now because up to a point the secular form of the Argument from Exile is *itself* recapitulated in the Argument from Alienation, one might wonder whether the same strategy will work here. It will not—because precisely where the Argument from Alienation *departs* from this recapitulation, what it resembles is the Argument from *Creativity*.

To put the same point without all of this cross-indexing, Kojève's hostility to Nature has more in common with Nietzsche's than with Kant's. Indeed, Kojève's ruminations on the "end of history" strongly evoke a speech on the "last men" that Nietzsche puts into the mouth of his fictional alter ego. "Thus spoke Zarathustra" in the Prologue to the work of the same title:

> Alas, the time is coming when man will no longer shoot the arrow of his longing beyond man, and the string of his bow will have forgotten how to whir! . . .

> Alas, the time is coming when man will no longer be able to give birth to a star. Alas, the time of the most despicable man is coming, he that is no longer able to despise himself. Behold, I show you the *last man*.

> "What is love? What is creation? What is longing? What is a star?" thus asks the last man, and he blinks. . . .

> "Formerly, all the world was mad," say the most refined, and they blink. . . .

> "We have invented happiness," say the last men, and they blink.[20]

Because of the resemblance between the Arguments from Creativity and from Alienation, and because the Argument from Creativity has already been refuted, I would like to say that what is sauce for the goose is once again sauce for the gander—and it would be true; but ironically, the Argument from Creativity is superior to the Argument from Alienation. Nietzsche believed that the only unambiguous contribution of Nature to the effort to "overcome" oneself and become what one *can* become is the creative impulse itself. Although I disagree that it *is* creative in his sense of the term and disagree that it is the *only* contribution of Nature to self-overcoming, the only important point here is that this is one *more* contribution than Kojève recognizes.

The fundamental error of the Argument from Alienation is to take what is undeniably natural for the other animals as natural also for human beings; but unlike the other animals, we are characteristically endowed with impulses that *prevent* us from finding ease or satisfaction in the merely animal development of our other impulses. In fact, for us, under natural conditions, animal development is scarcely possible; excluding individuals who have been raised by wolves, anyone who can sink into sensuality without a trace is surely a masochist on another level, because this is the most brutal of all repressions. Precisely these impulses make us the only animals for whom a distinction can be drawn between the characteristic and the typical; precisely these also force us to subsume the full and appropriate *as well as* the characteristic under the heading "natural." Precisely these impulses are at the bottom of Kojève's otherwise inexplicable distaste for the prospect of our reintegration with the other animals, and precisely these also make a *permanent* and *universal* end to history (in Kojève's sense of the term) impossible. Any strong movement in such a repressive direction must eventually engender an equally violent reaction, as in this country we may yet have the misfortune to learn. I return to some of these issues later under the rubric of the "critique" of Nature.

CHAPTER TWO

The Unity of Nature (1)

Chapter 2 resumes the reconstruction of the concept of
human nature where the middle sections of Chapter 1 left off.
Human flourishing requires that life have a certain rational
unity, in three respects. The rational unity of life as an unfolding chain of events—the first of these respects—is the
subject of this chapter.

The Problem of Rational Unity

A clear implication of the last chapter was that a flourishing
life has a certain *rational unity*. For instance, I argued that "the
rational activity by which we understand ourselves, bring our
lives into purposeful order, and keep them in this order" is the
mark of our full and appropriate development as human beings.
But just how should this be taken? The object of the next two
chapters is to spell out the meaning of "rational unity" in greater
detail. First, I will ask what we could possibly mean by the
rational unity of a *whole life*, when every life is strung out in
episodes along the cord of passing time. Second, I will ask what
we could possibly mean by the rational unity of *character*, when
every personality is a mass of different parts and passions.
Third, I will ask what we could possibly mean by the rational
unity of *motive*, when the way in which we decide what to do is
so different from the way in which we explain the choice to
others—or even to ourselves. Answering these questions should

prepare the way for the account of the virtues offered in the Mezzalogue.

The Rational Unity of a Whole Life

The artistic metaphor of the Argument from Creativity may provide us with a starting point: to elucidate the rational unity of a whole life, we may ask into what genre of art the crafting of a human life falls. Sculpture—the answer Nietzsche seemed to presuppose—is the wrong answer, because statues are forever the same; they may unfold to us *subjectively* as we walk around them, but temporality is not intrinsic to the works themselves. Now rational beings of such fixity can certainly be conceived; indeed, Thomas Aquinas so conceived the angels. He believed that although angels are changeable in some respects—possessing the powers of intellect, choice, and movement—they are unchanging in essence. Whatever one may think of the possibility of this mode of being, though, it isn't ours; we are embedded neither in "eternity" nor in "aeviternity" but in "time."[1] To be sure, we may suspect that the way in which an agent's life unfolds in time may not tell his *whole* story; Kant, for example, thought that our belief that we are responsible for our choices strongly compels the suspicion that there *is* more to us, because the only thing we can see in time is "cause" and "effect." But there is no need to take a position on that issue here. The point is that *so far as consciousness can disclose our Nature to us at all*, we are a kind of being that unfolds.

If sculpture is not our genre because statues do not unfold, then by the same token, painting is not our genre either. What products of art do unfold? Plans unfold, as do melodies, dances, plays, poems, and stories. Insofar as the last five have rational content, they can be considered media of narration, which leaves us with only plans and narratives. Thus we can revise our genre question: is the rational unity of a whole life more like the unity of a plan or the unity of a narrative?

Neither of these alternatives originates with this book. The first proposal, that the rational unity of a whole life is of the same kind as the unity of a plan, is implicit in an account of human good given in John Rawls's *Theory of Justice*.[2] The second, that the rational unity of a whole life is of the same kind as the unity of a narrative, has been most vigorously advanced by Alasdair MacIntyre in his *After Virtue*.[3] Each writes as though his conception of the rational unity of a whole life were the only one possible—in fact, each thinks that his conception is the very one which is latent in a tradition of theorizing that begins with Aristotle. I will discuss each in turn, beginning with MacIntyre, and then compare them.

The Narrative Hypothesis

MacIntyre proposes "a concept of a self whose unity resides in the unity of a narrative which links birth to life to death as narrative beginning to middle to end." A little later he elaborates by saying that "the concept of a person is that of a character abstracted from a history," a history being "an enacted dramatic narrative in which the characters are also the authors." Elsewhere this is qualified with the remark that we are "never more (and sometimes less)" than co-authors. This deeply limits what we can sensibly do or say; however, it does not undercut our accountability to one another, because accountability means precisely being able to give an *account*—a narrative account—of "what one did or what happened to one or what one witnessed at any earlier point"; and we are open to giving accounts to one another precisely *because* our narratives "interlock." I am the subject of my narrative but also a character in yours; you are the subject of your narrative but also, possibly, a character in mine.[4]

Since MacIntyre realizes that the narrative conception of the self may be unfamiliar, he undertakes to show "how *natural* it is to think of the self in a narrative mode."[5] This demonstration seems to have five parts.

First, "we cannot . . . characterize behavior independently of intentions."[6] This is because behavior performed with one intention is not the same behavior as that performed with another intention, even if the two are outwardly identical. When we ask what a man is doing, we want more than a description of his bodily motions and their effects.

Second, we cannot adequately characterize intentions themselves without reference to both their causal and their temporal order. Regarding their causal order, "we need to know which intention or intentions were primary, that is to say, of which it is the case that, had the agent intended otherwise, he would not have performed that action." Regarding their temporal order, "we need to know what the longer and longest-term intentions are and how the shorter-term intentions are related to the longer," for "each of the shorter-term intentions is, and can only be made, intelligible by reference to some longer-term intentions; and the characterization of the behavior in terms of the longer-term intentions can only be correct if some of the characterizations in terms of shorter-term intentions are also correct."[7]

Third, we cannot adequately characterize intentions "independently of the settings" in which they occur, because these settings "make these intentions intelligible both to agents themselves and to others." The term "setting" is here used broadly to include any kind of human "milieu" at all.[8]

But fourth (concerning the second point), we cannot characterize the causal and temporal order of an agent's intentions except "with reference to their role in his or her history."[9]

And fifth (concerning the third point), the setting itself has a history, "a history within which the histories of individual agents not only are, but have to be, situated, just because without the setting and its changes through time the history of the individual agent and his changes through time will be unintelligible."[10]

This concludes MacIntyre's demonstration: "Narrative history of a certain kind turns out to be the basic and essential genre for the characterization of human actions." Conversations, for instance, "have beginnings, middles and endings just as do literary works. They embody reversals and recognitions; they move toward and away from climaxes. There . . . may be digressions and subplots, indeed digressions within digressions and subplots within subplots." And what is true of conversations, he says, is true of "transactions" in general.[11]

Similar claims have been hotly debated in the field of literary criticism and in some of the social sciences, as MacIntyre is well aware. Against those writers who say that the structure of a narrative is imposed upon events only in retrospect, so that many stories—all essentially different—can be told about the same sequence of actions, he makes two points. In the first place, "certainly we must agree that it is only retrospectively that hopes can be characterized as unfulfilled or battles as decisive and so on. But we so characterize them in life as much as in art." In the second place, the multiplicity of stories that *can* be told about a given sequence of actions does not prevent us from asking, "What kind of account . . . will be both true and intelligible?" Thus he does not agree that "stories are not lived but told." Rather, he argues that "stories are lived before they are told—except in the case of fiction."[12] Thus "man is in his actions and practice, as well as in his fictions, essentially a story-telling animal. He is not essentially, but becomes through his history, a teller of stories that aspire to truth."[13]

A final thesis is that in all lived narratives, two characteristics coexist that look at first as though they would be incompatible. The first is "a kind of unpredictability": "we do not know what will happen next." The second is a "partial teleology": "We live out our lives . . . in the light of certain conceptions of a possible shared future." Putting the two together, "it is always both the case that there are constraints on how the story can continue *and* that within those constraints there are indefinitely many ways that it can continue." In the end, though, the second characteristic is more important than the first. Since we always see ourselves as moving or failing to move toward certain ends or goals, the unity of life is not the unity of just *any* kind of narrative but the unity of a narrative "quest"—specifically, a quest for "the" good by which the other partial goods in our lives can be ordered.[14]

The Plan Hypothesis

"A person," says Rawls, "may be regarded as a human life lived according to a plan," for "an individual says who he is by describing his purposes and causes, what he intends to do in his life."[15] This idea figures centrally in Rawls's account of human good, the thrust of which is that "a person's good is determined by what is for him the most rational long-range plan of life given reasonably favorable conditions." "To put it briefly," he says,

"the good is the satisfaction of rational desire,"[16] and what makes
a desire rational is just that it is "encouraged and provided for by
the plan that is rational for him."[17] Thus everything depends
upon knowing what makes an individual's choice of life-plan
rational.

In Rawls's view, the single formal principle that best characterizes the rational choice of a life-plan is "to adopt that plan
which maximizes the expected net balance of satisfaction."[18] He
goes to some lengths to show that he is not simply advocating
hedonism. What he finds objectionable in hedonism is the assumption that all satisfactions are comparable in terms of the
quantity of pleasurable sensation they yield. Nevertheless, he
clearly agrees with hedonism in two important points. First, he
agrees that the exercise of reason is a means to the end of choosing a life-plan, not an end in itself: "There is even nothing irrational in an aversion to deliberation . . . provided that one
is prepared to accept the consequences."[19] Consequently, he
stresses the *hypothetical* character of the choice of a life-plan. An
individual's good is determined by the plan he *would* choose in a
full exercise of reason. There is no need to assume that he *does* or
should so choose; therefore, "the limit decision to have no plan at
all, to let things come as they may, is still theoretically a plan
that may or may not be rational."[20] Second, Rawls agrees with
the hedonist that whether or not different satisfactions are comparable, there is no other criterion for the choice of a life-plan *but*
its anticipated satisfactions.

Now the fact that a plan of life is long-term does not imply
that it is a "detailed blueprint for action." That is, although it
will "make some provision for even the most distant future and
for our death," still "it becomes relatively less specific for later
periods." Thus it amounts to "a hierarchy of plans, the more
specific subplans being filled in at the appropriate time." Besides
consisting of a hierarchy of subplans, it also "mirrors a hierarchy
of desires proceeding in similar fashion from the more to the less
general." Putting these two features together, Rawls concludes
that "planning is in part scheduling. We try to organize our
activities into a temporal sequence in which each is carried on for
a certain length of time." The object is to find that plan "which
best organizes our activities and influences the formation of our

subsequent wants so that our aims and interests can be fruitfully combined into one scheme of conduct."[21]

The last remark calls for elaboration because it implies that "we can choose now which desires we shall have at a later time." Rawls admits that this may at first seem implausible, but he insists that "we can certainly decide now to do something that we know will affect the desires we shall have in the future," such as following a certain career. So he concludes that we can indeed "choose between future desires" and do so "in the light of our existing desires."[22]

Now, *because* different satisfactions cannot all be weighed on a single scale of sensation, the principle of choosing just that life-plan which maximizes the expected net balance of satisfaction "fails to provide us with an explicit procedure for making up our minds."[23] Rawls's response to this problem has two parts.

In the first place, a certain explicit procedure *can* be used to narrow the set of all possible life-plans into a certain "maximal class."[24] This procedure can be summarized in three principles. The first is the principle of effective means: given an objective, choose the plan that realizes it in the best way, provided that the plans are otherwise neutral. The second is the principle of inclusiveness: "one . . . plan is to be preferred to another if its execution would achieve all of the desired aims of the other and one or more further aims in addition."[25] The third is the principle of greater likelihood, which applies only when the aims intended by two plans are the same: if "some objectives have a greater chance of being realized by one plan than the other, yet at the same time none of the remaining aims are less likely to be attained," the first plan is to be preferred.[26]

The life-plans remaining after these principles have been applied are not necessarily equally good, but the explicit means of comparing them have been exhausted. At this point Rawls resorts to what he calls "full deliberative rationality." Full deliberative rationality is a certain activity undertaken by an individual with a certain competence. The requisite competence seems to have three parts. First, the individual "knows the general features of his wants and ends both present and future, and he is able to estimate the relative intensity of his desires, and to decide if necessary what he really wants." This means that "when he achieves his aim, he does not find that he no longer wants it and wishes that he had done something else instead."[27] Second, "he can envisage the alternatives open to him and establish a coherent ordering of them: given any two plans he can work out which one he prefers or whether he is indifferent between them, and these preferences are transitive." That he *can* envisage the alternatives means that the future can be "accurately foreseen and adequately realized in the imagination." Third, "once a plan is settled upon, he is able to adhere to it and he can resist present temptations and distractions that interfere with its execution." Possessed of this competence, the individual considers "what it would be like to carry out" each plan of life in the maximal class, in order to ascertain which one "would best realize his more fundamental desires."[28] Since the principles of effective means, inclusiveness, and greater likelihood have no further use, here he must be his own judge of the meaning to be given the word "best."

The Narrative and Plan Hypotheses Compared

The differences between the concept of a lived narrative and the concept of a life-plan are quite obvious. (a) In the first, rationality of a certain kind has intrinsic value because it is a function of authorship; in the second, it has value only as a means to the end of satisfaction. (b) The unity of the first is an emerging unity, while the unity of the second is preordained; thus the second would rule out such things as honest changes of heart. (c) The first portrays us as implicated in one another's efforts to make sense of ourselves; according to the second, we are related to one another only through the objects of common desire—over which we are in conflict. (d) Room can be found in the first for motives that grow directly out of the dramatic quality of the story, whereas there are no motives in the second that are not reducible to the impulses of desire. In all these respects, the concept of a lived narrative seems to be richer and more convincing than the concept of a life-plan.

Then again, in other respects the concept of a lived narrative and the concept of a life-plan are quite similar. For instance, MacIntyre's treatment of the temporal and causal order of human intentions has its counterpart in Rawls's remarks on the hierarchy of timed subplans and the hierarchy of desires, and here Rawls's account is certainly tidier. In addition, we certainly do *both* tell stories *and* make plans. The question is which is fundamental, and which incidental. If one can be embedded in the other, it may be irrelevant which is richer.

Now it is clear that nothing prevents a character in a narrative from making a plan. Plans, then, can be embedded in narratives. What may be less clear is that a plan *must* be embedded in a narrative to have meaning or even to exist. The self-subsistent plan is impossible. Several considerations support this conclusion.

The first is obvious, but telling. The rational choice of a plan of life does not come out of nowhere; rather, the individual making the choice has an antecedent history. The more Rawls tries to banish this history at the beginning of his account, the more he is compelled to sneak it back in later by allowing the chosen plan to become "relatively less specific for later periods."

The second consideration is that plans sufficiently encompassing for an entire life surpass the powers of human, or even temporal, reason—even if in matters of detail they *do* become "relatively less specific for later periods." Whereas MacIntyre conceives a "partial" teleology coexistent with "a kind of" unpredictability, so that "it is always both the case that there are constraints on how the story can continue *and* that within those constraints, there are indefinitely many ways that it can continue," Rawls wants to say that in all the *important* features of the plan, teleology is total and unpredictability can be reduced to zero. He is certainly right to point out that we make decisions to do things that we know will affect the desires we will have in the future, but as to *how* those desires will be affected, we can never have more than a vague and fallible idea. Not even infinite analytical intelligence could serve us here; it is a theorem in the mathematics of automata that no computational device can predict its own future state.[29] In order to know our own future, we would have to be there already looking at it, like God; and in this case, we would no longer be talking about beings that unfold.

The last consideration is that certain features of Rawls's own account seem to point to the embedding of plans in lived narratives. These features are two *additional* constraining principles that he injects into the discussion of full deliberative rationality without warning. Both principles are related to time.

The first is the principle of continuity. "The whole plan," Rawls explains, "has a certain unity, a dominant theme. There is not, so to speak, a separate utility function for each period. Not only must effects between periods be taken into account, but substantial swings up and down are presumably to be avoided."[30] There is an odd tension here. "Utility" is clearly a planning concept; here it means essentially the same thing as "net balance of satisfaction." "Theme," by contrast, is just as clearly a narrative concept. This does not seem to be a fluke, for although the importance of considering the effects of one period upon another can be explained in terms of maximizing the expected net balance of satisfaction, the importance of avoiding substantial swings up and down *exclusive* of their interperiod effects cannot be so explained.

The second time-related principle, which Rawls does not name, might be called the principle of rising expectations: "Other things being equal, we should arrange things at the earlier stages so as to permit a happier life at the later ones." The first puzzling thing about this principle is that it seems to contradict a stricture Rawls emphasizes only a paragraph earlier, that "mere temporal position, or distance from the present, is not a reason for favoring one moment over another."[31] Because the moment in time during which a satisfaction is rendered is irrelevant to the net balance of satisfaction over a whole life, Rawls has good reasons for emphasizing this stricture. But how can he square it with the principle of rising expectations?

"We might try to explain" the principle, he says, "by the relatively greater intensity of the pleasures of anticipation over those of memory." There is no time to wonder why the pleasures of anticipation should be more intense than the pleasures of memory, for the suggestion that they are is no sooner offered than dropped. "Even leaving this element aside," he continues, "the rising or at least the nondeclining plan appears preferable, since later activities can often incorporate and bind together the results and enjoyments of an entire life into one coherent structure as those of a declining plan cannot." Is this true? Of course it is. But although from a planning perspective, it is proper to *weigh up* the results and enjoyments of an entire life, the "incorporating" and "binding together" of which Rawls here speaks cannot be justified in those terms. What they suggest instead is the culmination of a story. Thus, even by Rawls's account, we seem to have not a self-subsistent plan but a plan embedded in a lived narrative.

An objection to this entire discussion may yet be drawn from the fact that not all narratives *do* possess the kind of unity that has been claimed for them here. Some of the works of literary modernists possess very little in the way of beginning, middle, or end, to say nothing of "incorporating" or "binding together." Well, that is true enough. Not all lives have this kind of unity either. But the kind of unity that a *told* narrative *may* have, is the same as the kind that a *lived* narrative *must* have. For told narratives without the kind of unity I describe may have uses in illuminating the disunities of the lives we actually lead, thereby helping us to achieve the unity we lack (or so I imagine that a literary modernist would argue). But though a Kafka story may reveal something about certain lives, that is not to say that life should be modeled on a Kafka story.

Provisional Conclusion

One of our hypotheses has clearly fared better than the other. Then should we mark down as "proven" the hypothesis that the rational unity of a whole life is of the same kind as the rational unity of a (true) narrative (with embedded plans)? We might do this and then conclude that we had learned something about human nature, but we had better go further, because MacIntyre himself denies it.

This is unexpected, to say the least. When MacIntyre says that

> man is in his actions and practices, as well as in his fictions, essentially a story-telling animal [but that] he is not essentially, but becomes through his history, a teller of stories that aspire to truth,

one is *tempted* to take this as meaning that

> man is innately so endowed that in his actions and practice, as well as in his fictions, he is characteristically a story-telling animal (and

that) although he is not characteristically a teller of stories that
aspire to truth, he becomes one as part of his full and appropriate
development.

But this is not what MacIntyre means at all. He turns down
ethical naturalism flat, calling it a "metaphysical biology."[32]

That he should make such a charge is doubly odd. A metaphysical biology was certainly presupposed in the naturalism of
Aristotle; MacIntyre is right about that. But in the first place, as
I have already shown, naturalism can be reconstructed *without*
Aristotle's metaphysics—a thought that does not seem to occur
to him. In the second place, rather than attempting to maintain a
metaphysical neutrality, MacIntyre simply winds up by replac-
ing metaphysical biology with metaphysical *history*, or so it
seems to me. One even suspects that when he uses the term
"essence," he really means something like the Hegelian historical
essence. And ultimately the historical gambit fails him; a good
case can be made that his argument is riddled, despite his anti-
naturalistic convictions, with tacit assumptions about the full
and appropriate development of human powers. And where
MacIntyre *is* faithful to the historical gambit, it leads him into
circularities, as when he tries to say that "the good life for man is
the life spent in seeking the good life for man" and that "a living
tradition" is an argument "precisely in part about the goods
which constitute that tradition."[33] Thus we slide out of the lap of
history and ask again: have we really learned something about
human nature, or rather something about—well, something
else?

I think that we have learned something about human nature.
Earlier, I suggested that we reach the truth about our full and
appropriate development in a reflective equilibrium *conditioned*
by our characteristic impulses and by what we know about
them. But that suggests a procedure we would do well to follow
now. The hypothesis that the rational unity of a whole life is of
the same kind as the rational unity of a true narrative has already
been successfully recommended to reflection. What I must show
next is that this success was no accident. MacIntyre was right
beyond his intention when he stressed "how natural" it is to
think of the self in a narrative mode. I will try to corroborate this

remark by examining the psychological processes of representation and self-representation.

The first of the following two sections is devoted almost entirely to definition and distinction. This may seem a digression from the subject of the chapter, but sometimes the shortest distance between two points is not a straight line. Some readers may prefer to skip the next section on a first reading of the chapter, and return later to beat the bushes.

The Concept of Cognitive Mapping

Among the various kinds of learning, a broad distinction can be made. In one group are forms of learning where what is learned is always immediately evident in behavior, so that we may speak strictly in terms of associations between stimuli and responses without bringing internal processing into the picture. A few obvious examples are classical and operant conditioning.

"Behaviorists" in the mold of B. F. Skinner believe that all learning is like this. However, very few behaviorists are left anymore, because some forms of learning are *not* always immediately evident in behavior, and in cases like this there is really no alternative but to assume that information has been reorganized within the nervous system. A mockingbird may hear another bird's song, then go on about its usual behaviors without giving any outward sign that it has learned anything at all. The same stimuli elicit the same responses as before. But the next day, or the day after, it may suddenly produce a perfect copy of the other bird's song on the very first try. What ethologists believe today is that when the mockingbird listens to the other bird's song, it converts what it hears into "target values" against which its own auditory responses will be matched at some later time by means of a very rapid feedback and control system. This is called "two-stage *sollwert* learning," after the German word for "target value." In the first stage the target values themselves are learned, without any behavioral indication that this has taken place; in the second stage the target values are called out of storage in order to "set" the feedback and control system so that the song itself can be learned.

Now another process that involves internal reorganization is *thinking*, but this term takes in so many different things that to say anything helpful about it without breaking it down a bit is probably impossible. One of the activities into which thinking can be broken down is "cognitive mapping" or, as I will call it, "mapping," without the adjective. This is the activity that will concern us for the rest of the chapter.

Mapping can be defined as the process by which *representations of relationships* are made, modified, and stored within the central nervous system. That it goes beyond the mere mechanical recording of sensory impulses may go without saying. But that might also be said of processes much more elementary than mapping: some processing of sensory impulses takes place in the sensory organs before the impulses ever reach the brain, and some secondary processing takes place in the more primitive parts of the brain itself. Mapping is the subordination of what comes *out* of such processes to higher-order systems of organization, which we develop and revise as we go along. For instance, the ability to recognize the borders of the objects in our visual fields is made possible by preliminary processing in the retina and the optic nerves. "There is a border here" is not something the rods and cones tell us by themselves. But although border recognition is a *prerequisite* of being able to situate ourselves with respect to the objects in our visual fields, it is no more than that. Situating ourselves requires a feat of much higher order: the development of a locational map.

Of course, some of our mapping processes involve interaction with other persons, and it is also likely that the ways we put together our maps have some influence on the processes that feed them data in the first place. A simple example is that sometimes we see what we expect to see, learn what we expect to learn, and feel what we expect to feel—by virtue of having expected it. But we don't do this always—and never (one hopes) entirely. I say "we," by the way, because whether *any* animals besides human beings are able to map is a hotly contested question in the scientific world. That they do it is not an easy thing to prove. For instance, just because a termite has learned to run a maze, we are not entitled to say that somewhere in its nervous system the termite must have stored a representation of the spatial relationships involved in the maze. It may simply have learned a mechanical sequence of operations. Likewise, bees who can always find their way to the hive may simply possess an efficient set of "orientation responses." Current thinking seems to be that rats map mazes and termites don't, but this is a matter for specialists.[34]

Another matter for specialists is determining just what neurological mechanisms are involved in mapping. However, one or two points about them are germane here. To begin with, the representation of relationships requires kinds of memory different from those that many other kinds of internal reorganization require. Consider the relationships that are involved in instrumental thinking, relationships like "cause to effect" and "means to end." These could never be represented at all unless the organism's memory were both *temporal* and *affective*. It would have to be temporal because an essential aspect of instrumental relationships is the difference between before and after. It would have to be affective because, unless the organism remembered not only previous experiences but also the feelings that these experiences evoked, the memory of the experiences would be irrelevant to present desire. Perhaps the only reason we evolved feelings was so that we *could* remember them. Theology might suggest other reasons, but the theory of natural selection would be hard put to do so.

Besides spatial and instrumental relationships, a great many other kinds of relationships can be mapped, but probably the most important of these is the relationship of *signification*. The way in which we deal with signification makes all the difference between what I intend to call *witting* and *unwitting* mapping; that, in turn, makes much of the difference between human beings and other animals that map (or seem to map).

Signification is the relationship in which something is a *sign* of something else—fact, quality, condition, or object—which is not immediately evident. For instance, the aroma of food is a sign that dinner is ready (a fact); the odor of brimstone is a sign of combustibility (a quality); a buoyant stride is a sign of high spirits (a condition); and tobacco smoke is a sign of a friend who has just departed (for purposes of this illustration, an object). Precisely because signification *is* a relationship, only an organism that maps can recognize signs. This deserves emphasis because the recognition of a sign may lead to behavior that is *functionally* equivalent to the response to a stimulus, yet they are not the same thing. A cockroach and a greedy man may both run toward the aroma of food, but that is no excuse for saying that the cockroach, like the man, recognizes the aroma as a sign that food is nearby.

Some signlike stimuli are very complex; an example is the dance that bees perform after returning from scouting, which causes other bees to fly in just the direction that will take them to the flowers that the scouts have found. Scientists devise ingenious experiments with the idea of determining whether various signs are true or bogus, but which are which is immaterial to my argument so long as the difference between them is understood in principle.

Signs also differ among themselves in other important ways. Both true signs and bogus can be *conventionalized;* both true signs and bogus can be *exchanged;* and although bogus signs cannot be exchanged *intentionally*, true signs can be. Now among true signs that are both conventionalized and intentionally exchanged, I would like to draw special attention to a certain group of them, which may be called *symbols.* Since the term "symbol" is used in so many different senses, I am a bit leery of introducing it here, but no other term is quite suitable and I will try to be very precise. As I use the term, symbolism is a special kind of signification that involves a special kind of map.

This point had best be approached indirectly. One is often struck in speaking with children that they do not realize what a difference there is between the world and their descriptions of the world. They do not understand signs as telling about their maps at all, but as telling about the world itself. So far as they know, maps are not "about" the world; they "are" the world. As it were, thinking is being—an intermediate term in the chain of signifiers is missing from their awareness. If we use the term "reference" for the self-conscious use of signs to say something *about a map* which is in turn about the world, then we might say that children have simply caught on to signifying in general more thoroughly than they have caught on to referring.

Without knowing this about children, we might easily have made the mistake of thinking that *all* signifying is referring.

Since not all of it is, we ought to distinguish signs that refer from signs that do not refer; and signs that refer are just that subclass of conventionalized and intentionally exchanged signs that were called "symbols" a moment ago. Clearly, using a sign *as a symbol* requires that one be able to tell the difference between world and map, and that is what is most important here.

One more piece of terminology will be useful. The kind of mapping that we do when we are conscious of the difference between world and map I will call *witting*, while the kind of mapping that we do when we are unconscious of the difference I will call *unwitting*. The power to map *wittingly* is what makes it possible for us not merely to fight but to *disagree*; not merely to suffer conflicting responses to a single stimulus situation but to *doubt*; not merely to be attracted by novel stimuli but to be *curious*. But from the fact that we can map wittingly, it does not follow that *all* of our mapping is witting; in fact, probably very little of the mapping that we perform, even as adults, is witting. To distinguish map from world in all things would be an oddly metaphysical vocation if it were possible at all. Yet even our unwitting mapping must be different from whatever unwitting mapping could be performed by creatures that could *only* map unwittingly. Even when the difference between map and world slips from our minds, we cannot help fashioning our maps by the same tools we use when we *are* conscious of the difference. After their most obvious use, we call these tools "linguistic." And so it is that every thought—even if unexpressed—is full of grammar and figure. If, like the Greeks of the classical period, we used the same word for reason as for speech, we could not be far wrong.

The Provisional Conclusion Revisited

I remarked in the last section that we make cognitive maps of all kinds of things: the physical world, the social world, the personal world, and so forth. At the moment, I am making a map of our mapping processes. But nowhere was it suggested that all of these things are carefully measured out in one grand map, nor even that a few maps courteously divide the realm of things signified among them. In fact, this is quite wrong. We set stylus to many, many maps, plentiful as blackberries, and they cover wildly crisscrossing, overlapping, and gerrymandered territories; that is to say, dozens of different "thinking" processes go on within us all at the same time. I am my own witness in this, although I think that I can call as further witnesses any readers who are willing to risk introspection. Mind your thoughts, and the traces of feeling that they bear, closely, microscopically: you will not find still waters or a few connected pools but a frothing, foaming confluence. How difficult it is to keep track of our own motives, our own feelings, our own impulses, without deceiving ourselves!

In the end, of course, we do deceive ourselves. We have no choice, although there is a difference between the self-deception of the sane and the self-deception of the insane and neurotic. We maintain a very special cognitive map: a record, ideally *single*, *simplified*, and *continuous*, of the many, complex, and disjointed mental events that participate every time we think or do or feel something. This is an enormously powerful organizing device because all of the other processes that go on within us depend on it as though it were the *Encyclopedia Britannica*—or perhaps I should say the script of *Hamlet*, since just as we seem to be incapable of having a thought without grammar and figure, we seem to be incapable of maintaining a record without plot, theme, and tension. But since it overshadows all other records of experience, we have the impression that those many, complex, and disjointed mental events that participate every time we think or do or feel something *really are* single, simple, and continuous. The name for this impression is "consciousness." It makes us think that we are merely "egos." In a way, consciousness is real, although not in quite the way we think. Consciousness is an attribute of memory, not of experience; I may already be spinning it as I act, but it is always a fraction of a second behind. In a way, ego is real, although again not in quite the way that we think. Constantly calling upon a single, simple, and continuous record of experience does make our many, complex, and disjointed mental events unfold differently than they would otherwise, and gives them a certain coherency.

This can easily be misunderstood. Modern social theory, especially in its European varieties, has a strong iconoclastic strain. Always one wants to "dissolve the illusions" of something—for those who like Marx, the illusions of ideology; for those who like Nietzsche and Freud, the illusions of consciousness. A certain kind of social theorist, in fact, is happy to dissolve any illusions whatsoever. But one should always distinguish between the respect in which something *is* an illusion, and the respect in which it is *not*. Neither Marx nor Nietzsche did this consistently, and most of their followers do not do it at all.

One of Nietzsche's examples is revealing. Without knowing, I touch a flame. The sensory nerves in my hand send impulses up my arm to the spine. There, some of them complete a reflex arc so that a command is sent back down my arm instructing the muscles to contract, while others continue on up the spine to the brain. By the time the brain receives the impulses with which it will construct the sensation of pain, my arm has already been pulled from the flame. However, since the new sensory impulses caused by the movement of my arm also take time to travel up the arm and spine to the brain, I am aware of the pain before I am aware of the movement. Now that the sequence of events is complete, though, what do I *think* has happened? I *think* that I felt the pain first, and pulled back my hand *for that reason*. There, says Nietzsche, what could be more obvious? Act always comes *first;* intention *follows* as an interpretation, and a false one, at that.[35]

Behaviorists should be happy with this argument, since—as I explained before—they believe that all behavior can be explained in terms of the passive association of stimuli with responses without any internal processing. But as we saw there, even when we leave "thinking" out of consideration, this argument is rather far out of line with the facts; for instance, it cannot explain what a mockingbird is doing when it listens to another bird's song and surprises us the next day by duplicating it. Where "thinking" *is* concerned, it is even further out of line. Nietzsche himself found it impossible to maintain his position. We do not like to admit—he was fond of saying—how much life depends on error.[36] He was right, but on the previous line of argument, the error cannot make any difference to the act; therefore, how can anything depend on it? What he should have said is that I may be wrong in thinking that I pulled my hand from the flame because of the pain, but I will *certainly* be more careful around flames in the future.

We need a name for this very special cognitive mapping that produces a single, simplified, continuous record of the many, complex, disjointed mental events that participate every time we think or do or feel something. In a MacIntyrian spirit one might call it *narration*. However, there are two kinds of narration, and so far I have only discussed one—although in the act of discussing it, I have been doing the other. Just as in mapping generally, so here, I may be either forgetful or aware of the difference between world and map. In this case, that means the difference between the part of the world that I am, and the part of me that is my map of myself—the difference between the soul, and the ego. While I am actually spinning my narrative, *constructing* the ego that inhabits it, I am characteristically forgetful of the difference. Hence, unwitting narration may be called *constructive* narration. But when I am scrutinizing and interrogating my narrative, plumbing the depths of my experience and *challenging* my ego to show that it is not merely a mask, I am necessarily aware of the difference. Hence, witting narration may be called *deep* narration.

Deep narration is not the same as what literary theorists call "deconstruction." Rather, deconstruction is a misunderstanding of deep narration. The deconstructive analysis of a text or of a self is an attempt to unmask the pretensions of its author. Nietzsche, to whom deconstructionists acknowledge a great debt, recognized such an attempt as a "spiritualized cruelty" to self and to others, and was willing to accept it on these terms.[37] We should not be. Properly conceived, deep narration would more rightly be called *re*construction than deconstruction: it wants not to destroy but to make whole. It may unmask, but only as one changes the filthy dressing on a wound. It involves mercy as well as judgment, and its characteristic passions arise not from cruelty but from love, wonder, or spiritual distress, as the examples of Plato and St. Augustine show. The forms of our cooperation in constructive narration are called "culture" and include all of our social and political institutions, rituals, and myths. The forms of our cooperation in deep narration are called "higher culture" and include some some art, some psychotherapy, true religion, and the adequate study of politics.

One consideration remains. Concerned that for present purposes I speak of the "soul," or true self, only in terms of a pattern of conjectural events in the central nervous system, many readers (especially Christians) will wonder whether between the lines I am really denying the soul's existence. Because at the moment the temper of my profession is profoundly agnostic, many of my fellow professionals will regard the question as profoundly uninteresting and almost impertinent. As a Christian, of course, I cannot accept that judgment; and although this is not a work of Christian apologetics, I think I am obliged to take the question seriously.

I believe that the question arises from a suspicion that "spirit" and "matter" can have no essential connection with each other. But that suspicion is Gnostic, not Christian: if the doctrine of the Incarnation means anything, it means that such a suspicion is wrong. As C. S. Lewis has remarked, "God likes matter. He invented it."[38] And matter, one need hardly add, seems to be the idiom in which He has, for the time being, inscribed us. One need not go so far as to accept the Aristotelian definition of the soul as "the form of the body,"[39] which means roughly the pattern that makes a lump of flesh a human being—although some have: witness Thomas Aquinas.[40] But the soul is *at least* that, and one is free to consider it more.[41]

CHAPTER THREE

The Unity of Nature (2)

Chapter 3 continues the discussion of rational unity by applying the concept to the character of the agent, and to the
agent's motives for action.

The Rational Unity of Character

One may well wonder why I think that a problem of the
"rational unity of character" is still left, because presumably the
ideally single, simplified, continuous narrative record that is the
repository of the ego is competent to make sense of the dozens of
cognitive maps that crisscross around it. So it may be, but the
main problem the individual faces is not to calibrate his maps but
to control the interior world they describe. To be sure, the
solution to the first problem and the solution to the second problem depend on each other—the soldier depends on his map
when he enters disputed territory, and modifies it as a result of
his engagements there—but the second problem needs to be
considered on its own terms.

Plato was the first to address this problem, and the first to
consider solutions, too. He began by remarking how common it
is for an individual to suffer contrary impulses. But if the soul
were a unitary thing, this would be impossible, because no unitary thing can be characterized in contrary ways at one and the
same time. Therefore, rather than being unitary, the soul must
be composed of parts.[1] Up to this point, Plato relied only upon

73

the logical principle of "noncontradiction."[2] After this, he was more adventurous. For if the soul is composed of parts, then what I have called the problem of the rational unity of character is the problem of how these parts should be related to one another.

Plato's startling suggestion was that the impulses the soul contains are like the citizens that make up a city, and that the parts of the soul are like the classes into which the citizens are divided.[3] Leaving open the question of just how many of these classes there are, he singled out three for attention. The class of the soul that includes the impulses of "desire," he said, is like the class of the city whose members are concerned with mundane economic pursuits—"moneymaking." In turn, the class of the soul that includes the "spirited" impulses such as anger, shame, and indignation is like the city's "guardians," who combine the roles of soldiers and police. Finally, the class of the soul that includes the impulses of "speech" or "reason" is like the class of the city whose members have the wisdom to rule. Conflict in the soul, as in the city, can occur both within and between classes: within, as when desire contends with desire; between, as when desire is checked by shame. At last Plato argued that the classes of a well-ordered soul are related to one another in the same fashion as the classes of a well-ordered city. In a well-ordered city, the guardians are docile; they take orders from the wise instead of terrorizing the population for their own gratification. Likewise, the moneymakers realize that their kind of "know-how" is different from the wisdom involved in true statecraft, and they do not press their demands to the detriment of the city. By the same token, the soul itself is well-ordered when both spiritedness and desire acquiesce in the judgments of reason.

Now there are two ways in which all of this can be interpreted. According to one, the important thing is that reason should subordinate the rest of the soul, and the elaborate analogy between soul and city has no other purpose than to produce this conclusion. According to the other, the important thing is that the soul is like a city rather than like some other kind of ordered group, and the idea of reason ruling the soul can be appreciated only within this context. In the next sections I will briefly review David Hume's grounds for thinking that the idea of reason ruling the soul is simply absurd, and I will suggest that the idea Hume attacked was not the one Plato had in mind—and that I accept. Then I will try to explore the real point of the analogy between soul and city and relate it once more to the problem of the rational unity of character.

"The Rule of Reason" out of Context

Every rational creature, it is said, is obliged to regulate his actions by reason; and if any other motive or principle challenge the direction of his conduct, he ought to oppose it till it be entirely subdued or at least brought to a conformity with that superior principle.[4]

Hume's real target in deriding "the fallacy of all this philosophy"[5] was not Platonism but the version of ethical rationalism extant in his own day—although it is likely that he saw them as birds of a feather. What he objected to was the idea that reason *by itself* could act as a motivating principle, even to the point of subduing passion if necessary. His argument is among the pithiest on record, in part because Hume intended it to serve as the prelude to a different argument altogether, which was the main attraction. He wanted to show that we derive the distinction between vice and virtue from a moral "sense." Showing that we do *not* derive it from the faculty of reason seemed to him the appropriate way to begin.

Hume's argument has the movement of a wave. It dashes itself upon the rocks, recedes, then plunges once more upon the shore, this time attaining its goal. Sweeping claims alternate with equally sweeping qualifications.

In the first place, Hume says that reason is nothing but "the discovery of truth or falsehood" and that this truth or falsehood is discovered in only two realms: the abstract relations of our ideas, and the concrete relations of our experience. Now if moral distinctions *are* derived from reason, then it must be possible to discover truth or falsehood in the relations among our passions, motives, and actions. However, in his view experiences in these categories are "original facts and realities, complete in themselves," and imply "no reference to other" passions, motives, or actions. Therefore, although we often do pronounce passions, for instance, *right* or *wrong*, we cannot sensibly pronounce them true or false. Now wherever something can be pronounced true or false, reason has a certain power. In a process of thought, it can advance a proposition by affirming it or call a halt to a proposition by contradicting it. Here that power is lacking. Being neither true nor false, a passion can be neither produced by affirmation of reason nor prevented by contradiction of reason. Therefore, over passions, motives, and actions, reason "has no influence"; it is "perfectly inert."[6]

As so far stated, the argument is obviously open to objection. Hume admits it himself: "It may be said that though no will or action can be immediately contradictory to reason, yet we may find such a contradiction in some of the attendants of the actions." To see what he means, we might consider a case in which I insult you because I *judge* that you have insulted me. In the ordinary way of speaking ("which," Hume drily remarks, "philosophy will scarce allow of"), my action may indeed be pronounced reasonable or unreasonable, according to whether that *judgment* is true or false. And since this shows that passions, motives, and actions have "reference" to one another after all, it seems to destroy the preceding argument.

Hume's cool response is to construct a *new* argument under the pretense of qualifying the first one. He now says that reason may indeed "prompt" an action, but to do so it must "concur with" some passion, and even then it is only an "oblique" or "mediate" cause. For instance, reason "may excite a passion by informing us of something which is a proper object of it," or it may discover "the connection of causes and effects so as to afford us means of exerting" it.[7] In the example given a few lines ago, reason works in both of these ways. It excites my anger by informing me that you are a proper object of it, and it affords me means of exerting my anger by discovering a suitably insulting reply to your original remark. The potential motive here is provided by my capacity for anger. Reason does no more than activate and direct it.

Now this may have needed saying to Hume's contemporaries; it is an effective refutation of *one interpretation* of the notion that reason should rule the soul. Yet surely that interpretation is

76

extravagant. When we say that a man has the mastery of a spirited horse, we do not usually mean that he runs in the place of the horse or carries the horse on his back, but that he activates and directs the eagerness of the horse to run—which is precisely the role that Hume himself allots to reason in relation to the passions. The implications of his own argument contradict his famous remark that "reason is, and ought only to be, the slave of the passions, and can never pretend to any other office than to serve and obey them."[8] For if the passions are so defined as to include every possible impulse (as Hume defines them), then it is trivially true that nothing can oppose a passion save another passion (as he claims); yet what armament *is* there for contending passions but the judgments of reason? If reason can excite a passion by informing us of the existence of something that is a proper object of it, then surely it can also defuse or redirect a passion by informing us that its object is improper!

But the distinction raises an interesting question. What do we *mean* by "proper" and "improper"? The passions themselves cannot decide the matter, for what we are really asking is to what end they are to *be* activated and directed. This, I think, is the kind of question Plato meant his account of the rational unity of character to suggest. The metaphor of horse and rider in the preceding paragraph is, after all, his.[9] Far from suggesting that the faculty of "discovering truth and falsehood" could act as a motivating principle in its own right, Plato went out of his way to show that "reason" could do nothing about "desire" except in an alliance with "spiritedness." And the truest interpretation of those three agencies of the soul seems to be something like this: desire is a reaching-out to what seems good to sense and imagination, principally the pleasant and the beautiful; spiritedness is a collection of impulses that tend to protect the seeming good, even at the risk of losing everything; and reason is a faculty not only for discovering truth and falsehood but also for transforming desire into a reaching-out for what not only seems but really *is* good.

But in order to do so much as approach ideas like this, we need to return the notion of the mastery of reason to its context in the comparison of the soul with the city.

"The Rule of Reason" Returned to Context

The points I would like to make in this section emerge most clearly and easily from a comparison between Plato's account of the soul and another account from a recent and unexpected source. Lately, computer scientists have put a great deal of time and energy into the attempt to develop programs that mimic the functions of human intelligence. By way of echo, other scientists and philosophers (sometimes the same ones) have tried to understand human beings by comparing them with sophisticated computers. Not long ago Marvin Minsky, a M.I.T. computer scientist at the forefront of the artificial intelligence movement, surprised his colleagues by comparing mind and personality with another thing altogether. The comparison is found in an article on human memory published in a journal of cognitive science. I will quote liberally from its introductory paragraphs to forestall any suspicion that I am putting words in Minsky's mouth:

In this modern era of "information processing psychology" it may seem quaint to talk of mental states; it is more fashionable to speak of representations, frames, scripts, or semantic networks. But while I find it lucid enough to speak in such terms about memories of things, sentences, or even faces, it is much harder to do so to deal with feelings, insights, and understandings—and all the attitudes, dispositions, and ways of seeing things that go with them. We usually put such issues aside, saying that one must first understand simpler things. But what if feelings and viewpoints are the simpler things? If such dispositions are the elements of which the others are composed, then we must deal with them directly. So we shall view memories as entities that predispose the mind to deal with new situations in old, remembered ways—specifically, as entities that reset the states of the parts of the nervous system. Then they can cause that nervous system to be "disposed" to behave as though it remembers. This is why I put "dispositions" ahead of "propositions." . . .

One could say little about "mental states" if one imagined the Mind to be a single, unitary thing. Instead, we shall envision the mind (or brain) as composed of many partially autonomous "agents"—as a "Society" of smaller minds. This allows us to interpret "mental state" in terms of *subsets of the states of the parts of the mind.* To give this idea substance, we must propose some structure for that mental society. In fact, we'll suppose that it works much like any human administrative organization. . . .

This concept of partial state allows us to speak of entertaining *several partial states at once*—to the extent they do not assign different states to the same individual agents. And even if there is such a conflict, the concept may still be meaningful, if that conflict can be settled within the society. This is important because (we suggest) the local mechanisms for resolving such conflicts could be the precursors of what we know later as *reasoning*—useful ways to combine different fragments of knowledge.[10]

Were it not for the fact that his bibliography lists nothing written prior to 1949, one would think that Minsky had mined the texts of Plato and Aristotle for his basic ideas. Take the idea of putting "dispositions" ahead of "propositions," and Minsky's general intuitions about just what is "simpler" than what. In a sense closely related to his, dispositions, not propositions, are at the foundation of all classical moral theory. According to Aristotle, the interaction of Nature and experience first produces rough-and-ready dispositions that he calls simply "habits"; good habits, in turn, are the basis for highly cultivated dispositions that he calls "virtues" or "excellences." Only very late in an individual's moral development have propositions much part in shaping the dispositions, and even these are simply rough inductive generalizations about the conduct that can be expected of individuals who possess the virtues already.

By contrast, most *modern* moral theories place propositions ahead of dispositions. John Rawls, for instance, is willing to speak about the "virtues" but defines them as dispositions that are "regulated by higher-order desires, in this case a desire to act from the corresponding moral principles."[11] The substitution of the morality of principles for the morality of virtues is related to the rejection of human nature as the centerpiece of moral theory; but I will say no more about it here because I intend to discuss it later in this chapter, and later in the book.

At any rate, much more important is the idea of mind being an aggregate of smaller minds—minds that require social organization because they are specialized in function but that can nevertheless come into conflict, requiring the adjudication of something like "reason." "Mind" is really too small a word for such a thing. "Soul" is better, and immediately we think of Plato's comparison of the soul with the city. The greatest difference between Plato's account of the soul and Minsky's account of the "mind" is that although both compare this thing in which we have our being with a social organism, each compares it with a different kind of social organism. Plato compares the soul to a city, that is to say, a political community. Minsky, by contrast, supposes that it is "much like any human administrative organization."

From a moral point of view—and I do not mean to suggest that Minsky realized that his theory presupposes a moral point of view, for modern thought does not regard the moral point of view as the comprehensive point of view, as ancient thought did—this difference is very important. The rational unity of an administrative organization is found in the same characteristic as the rational unity of a political community—in its fitness for realizing its end, or ends. But the ends of the two are not alike. The end of the first is twice-over *external:* it is assigned *by* an outside authority, and sought *in* the outside world. In both of these respects, by contrast, the end of the second is *internal.* True, with good reason each of the classes of the city pursues different things, and lest I give an unwarranted impression of insularity, I should stress that although some of these things pertain only to the world within the city, others do pertain in important ways to the world outside. Yet the end of the city *as a city*—abstracting from the other things it may be—is found in a concurrence of sentiment among its classes. This end is neither assigned by an authority in the world outside nor sought there.

Of course, the question must be asked in *what* sentiment the classes of the city concur. If concurrence in anything at all, secured by any means, counted as rational unity, then it could not be distinguished from coercive unity—nor could the city be distinguished from an administrative organization after all, and indeed, this is the goal of the totalitarian state. Plato's reply is that the classes concur, out of the desire for their own good, in the subordination of the less to the more complete pursuits as they understand them. Reflection on this point suggests that it is no accident that whereas Plato evaluates the rational unity of the soul in terms of intrinsic values, Minsky characterizes it in terms of "usefulness."

There is a way to reconcile their accounts which does justice to Plato's intentions as a philosopher and Minsky's contrasting intentions as a scientist. For obvious reasons, Minsky's analogy, not Plato's, is appropriate for the design of mechanical servants that mimic the functions of human intelligence. For less obvious reasons, it is also appropriate to the consideration of the *evolution* of human intelligence: from the view of the theory of natural selection, the mind's ends *were* in a manner of speaking assigned from outside. If the mind were not organized in such a way as to facilitate certain functions like finding food, shelter, and mates, the organism bearing that mind would not pass on its genes. Therefore only certain kinds of genes were passed on, and only certain kinds of minds are left. But Plato's account, not Minsky's, is appropriate to reflection on our full and appropriate development as human beings. Naturally we will continue to eat and take shelter and reproduce and so forth. But nothing compels us to adopt the same supreme ends for ourselves today as were "in a manner of speaking" assigned to us during the long twilight of natural selection. Despite the charlatan claims of sociobiology, the starting point for thinking about our full and appropriate development is what we are like, not how we came to be like that. Knowledge of how we came to be like that is helpful *only* on such occasions as it may help us to see what we are like now, and these occasions may be a good deal more rare than we sometimes suppose.

This concludes the interpretation of the "rule of reason" in connection with the problem of the rational unity of character.

The Rational Unity of Motive

One more problem of rational unity remains, the problem of the rational unity of motive. This problem is fairly easy to characterize. Because we are naturally social beings—beings who can flourish only in social relationships in which to one degree or another we disclose ourselves to one another, and which are at the least pretty much what they appear to be—it is quite literally "good for us" to acknowledge responsibility to one another for our actions. And as I said earlier, responsible action is usually regarded as action I take for reasons that I can justify to myself and to others in precisely the same way. But what does that mean—"in precisely the same way"? As John M. Cooper has pointed, "An account of practical thinking might be either a theory about how practical conclusions, and the actions express- ing them, are arrived at, or a theory about how conclusions (however arrived at) can be justified, or at any rate explained; or it might be both of these."[12] But it is not easy for it to be "both of these" because the plain fact of the matter is that the kind of thinking we do when we are coming to conclusions is very often different from the kind of thinking we do when we are debating whether these conclusions are correct.

I am not speaking of the misrepresentation of motives that Machiavelli praised, when he said that "one must know . . . how to be a fine liar and hypocrite; and men are so simple-minded and so dominated by their present needs that one who deceives will always find one who will allow himself to be deceived," or when he argued that although it is not necessary for a Prince to have all the moral qualities, "it is certainly necessary to appear to have them."[13] On the contrary, I am even (and especially) think- ing of moral reasoning. Suppose I want to persuade you that my position on the abortion issue is correct (and perhaps persuade myself at the same time). I might suggest principles with which we both agree and then try to show that what I believe about abortion can be deduced from them as a conclusion. Perhaps I will succeed in this. Yet when I arrived at my position on abor- tion in the first place, probably I did not have these principles in mind at all, and odds are that my reasoning did not resemble deduction in the least. I may indeed have begun with a certain sort of "principle"—for instance, "I should try to put myself in the shoes of the parties who might face a decision about abortion or who might be affected by it"—but this sort of principle does not function like the premises in a deductive argument. Rather it *primes* my faculties by disposing my imagination, sympathy, and intellect to interact in a certain manner; it puts me in "the right frame of mind" or helps me to take "the right point of view."[14]

But what are we to make of the fact that I come to my conclu-

sions in one way and justify them in the other? If there is no
relationship at all between my "priming" principles and my "justifying" principles, then however sharply I contrast in other
ways with Machiavelli's Prince, I am equally hypocritical. There
must be *some* relation between my priming principles and my
justifying principles, and a very close one at that. But what is it?
This is the problem of the rational unity of motive.

I will try to show how the problem can be resolved by briefly
describing four possible views of the proper relationship between the way in which we justify practical conclusions and the
way in which we arrive at them in the first place. I do not claim
that these views exhaust the possibilities, but I think they are the
most important, and I have arranged them in an order that helps
bring out my theses. Let me begin by making something very
clear: the terms in which I discuss these four views—for that
matter, even the terms in which I have just defined the problem
of the rational unity of motive—presuppose the truth of certain
theses that are not fully explained until later in the book. An
example of these is the thesis that we are naturally social, for
otherwise, why should we *care* whether the way in which we
come to our practical conclusions bears any relation at all to the
way in which we justify them before each other? Hypocrisy, in
this case, is no objection. However, I do not think that the moral
presuppositions I make in these sections beg the question at
hand. Despite the moral language I use, it would certainly be
possible for my attempt to solve the problem of the rational unity
of motive to fail in some irreparable way, and this would certainly undermine my effort to recommend the goodness of rational unity to the intuition of the reader. (Of what use would it
be to posit a good that cannot be achieved?) That is why, despite
the fact that my discussion of the rational unity of motive is part
of my larger ontological project—the reconstruction of the concept of Nature—the grounds of the distinction between the four
views I present are not ontological. That is to say, their differences turn on other issues than whether they portray values as
objective. *All four* present them as objective.

Each view but the first is a response to the weakness of the one
that precedes it. The first two may be taken as providing alternative foundations for a "morality of principles," while the sec-

ond two may be taken as providing alternative foundations for a "morality of virtues"—giving the lie, I hope, to any idea that these terms are univocal. The idea is that we need principles and virtues alike. Our virtues are the carriers of our principles, the interpreters of our principles, and the executors of our principles. This is why so many of our shared understandings remain unspoken: transfinite numbers of them are yet unthought. They are latent in our temperaments, lying in wait in our dispositions.

Absolutism

In an "absolutist" morality of principles, there is no room for *priming* principles at all, because in this view the way in which we arrive at practical conclusions *ought* to follow the same pattern as the way in which we justify them to others—whether or not it usually does. The principles that guide ideal individuals to their practical conclusions are identical, in this view, to the principles by which they justify them to others, except that they have internalized them. In *both* contexts—decision and justification—the principles are employed deductively.

This view is not obviously wrong, but it is reasonable only if all of the following conditions are satisfied:

1 the set of all moral principles is small enough that in attempting to deduce practical conclusions from them, ordinary human reason is not overwhelmed;
2 taken together with the facts of the case, they are adequate to decision in every situation whatsoever, public and private;
3 finally, their application is straightforward—that is, they are so complete that they eliminate any need for supplementary exercises of judgment.

The difficulty is that not all three conditions can be satisfied at once. Consider the Ten Commandments as an example. I am not here concerned to affirm or deny their rightness, but to investigate how they could be used. They are widely regarded by ordinary moral reasoners as satisfying conditions one and two, but no one maintains that they satisfy condition three. For instance, although I am commanded to honor my father and mother, I am not given an exhaustive set of instructions for interpreting the operative verb, "honor." This is hardly trivial, for the requirements of honor to parents are by no means easy to interpret, especially when parents dishonor themselves, each other, or their children. So I must exercise judgment. Likewise, I am told that the correct English translation of the fifth commandment is *not* "Thou shalt not kill" but "Thou shalt not murder," raising the question whether all killing is murdering. When is it murder to take life in war, and when is it justified self-defense? Is it murder to take the life of a murderer? Again, I must exercise judgment. Therefore, even if objectively true and inviolable, this set of principles cannot be construed "absolutistically" in my sense of the term, and the same is true for every set of moral principles that has ever been proposed. Although many individuals might claim to be absolutists if the term were explained to them, there has never been a moral code that could be followed in an absolutistic way.

This may be no accident. It may have something to do with the very nature of logical argument on any subject whatsoever. Even in the austere realms of logic and mathematics, Gödel's famous "incompleteness" theorems have shown us that to enumerate a set of axioms or principles sufficient to decide the truth or falsehood of every proposition we might propose is simply impossible. It cannot be done. Not even an infinite number of axioms will suffice. Why we should expect greater decisiveness in the far more vexing realms of the concrete, why we should expect proofs in morality and politics that we may not expect even in the theory of numbers, this, I confess, is a mystery too deep for my penetration.

Of course, the limitations of deductive argument in mathematics do not lead us to doubt mathematics; nor should the limitations of deductive argument in morality lead us to doubt morality. But when we are up against these limits, we have to find another way beyond them. This prompts the second of the four views I am to discuss.

Contra-Absolutism

Whereas in the absolutist view there is no room for priming principles at all, in what I would like to call the "contra-absolutist" view there is no room for anything *but* priming principles. The idea is that (again, in precise contrast with absolutism) the way in which we justify our practical conclusions to others *ought* to follow the same pattern as the way in which we come to them in the first place, and in *neither* context—decision or justification—are the principles employed deductively. Thus, just as I begin thinking about what to do by using the priming principles to get myself into the "moral frame of mind" or the "moral point of view," I should persuade you to accept my conclusions by showing you that if you get into the same frame of mind, you will reach the same conclusions. This view has a strong affinity with traditional Kantian ethics as well as with the most recent work by theorists in the liberal moral and political tradition.

As the liberal theorist James S. Fishkin has pointed out, arguments that subscribe to the pattern I am calling contra-absolutist have a certain "inconclusiveness"[15] (though for different reasons than do absolutist, or deductive arguments). This is because we may reasonably disagree about the implications of "putting ourselves into others' shoes," or "doing unto others as we would have them do unto us," or, as Kant put it, "only acting in such a way that we can will the underlying maxim of each act to be a universal law." Fishkin's remark is an understatement. Some years ago, R. M. Hare composed an imaginary debate between himself and a Nazi over the question of the extermination of the Jews.[16] The horrifying thing is that the Nazi "won"—in the sense that although Hare continued to object to the extermination of the Jews, most readers agree that he failed to show that the Nazi could *not* reconcile their extermination with the moral point of view. And no wonder. Were we to ask a Nazi to put himself in the others' shoes, he might obligingly reply, "I pity the Jews, who must truly wish to die." Were we to ask him to do unto others as he would have them do unto him, he might reply, "Were I a Jew who lacked the courage to commit suicide, I would wish to be put to death by someone else." And were we to follow Kant in asking him to act only in such a way that he could will the underlying maxim of his act to be a universal law, he might reply, "For the reasons that I have already given you, I can easily will the extermination of the Jews to be a universal law, and that is why I support it with my whole heart as the law of my Reich." Although I think that there may be varieties of "inconclusiveness" that need not trouble us, this is not one of them: the problem is that merely taking the moral point of view *is no guarantee that one will reason morally.*

This might all be dismissed as intellectual game-playing were it not for Adolph Eichmann's testimony at his trial for Nazi war crimes. Hannah Arendt reports that at a certain point

> he suddenly declared with great emphasis that he had lived his whole life according to Kant's moral precepts, and especially according to a Kantian definition of duty. This was outrageous, on the face of it, and also incomprehensible, since Kant's moral philosophy is so closely bound up with man's faculty of judgment, which rules out blind obedience. The examining officer did not press the point, but Judge Raveh, either out of curiosity or out of indignation at Eichmann's having dared to invoke Kant's name in connection with his crimes, decided to question the accused. And, to the surprise of everybody, Eichmann came up with an approximately correct definition of the Categorical Imperative: "I meant by my remark about Kant that the principle of my will must always be such that it can become the principle of general laws."[17]

We should ask: Was Eichmann still a Kantian when he took upon himself the responsibility for carrying out the Final Solution? Eichmann himself told the court that at that point he had ceased to be a Kantian. Arendt agrees that strictly speaking he could not possibly at that point have been a Kantian, because he had condoned what no Kantian could condone: for Kant, the decisive issue would have been that "the thief or the murderer cannot conceivably wish to live under a legal system that would give others the right to rob or murder him." But then she qualifies Eichmann's confession of apostasy from Kant by suggesting that *unconsciously* "he had not simply discarded the Kantian formula as no longer applicable, he had distorted it to read: Act as if the principle of your actions were the same as that of the legislator or of the law of the land."[18]

At both points Arendt seems to be in error. As we saw in the preceding paragraph, with a sufficiently distorted character one *can* wish to live under a legal system that would give others (given the hypothetical circumstance of his being a Jew) the right to rob or murder him. Given the distortion in Eichmann's character, it is unnecessary to suppose that he had unconsciously misread the categorical imperative, for even on a strict reading—wicked as he was—he could have justified the Final Solution to himself.

Whether this is what he actually did, we cannot know. His declaration that he had fallen away from his Kantian principles can be given no more credence than the other descriptions he gave of his motives. Thus we turn from Eichmann to Kant himself. Surely Kant would have been appalled by the enormity of Eichmann's evil, and we cannot hold him responsible for it. Yet his philosophy does not provide us with the means to understand that evil. For Kant, virtue was summed up in the possession of a "good will," which in turn is nothing more than a constant will to act consistently with the categorical imperative. But this raises the central problem of contra-absolutism. The moral point of view is no good without excellence of character, but contra-absolutism refuses to define excellence of character in any terms *other than* the readiness to take the moral point of view.

Although Fishkin does not discuss evil on the scale of Eichmann's, he does admit that the "inconclusiveness" of contra-absolutist arguments can be awkward. Pointing to the fact that many recent liberal theorists have tried by one means or another to "tighten" the definition of the moral point of view, notably John Rawls in his well-known *Theory of Justice*, Fishkin expresses the hope that the inconclusiveness of contra-absolutist arguments can be reduced to tolerable levels.[19] One may ask why he does not propose eliminating the inconclusiveness altogether. The reason, as he points out, is simply that one can go only so far in reducing the inconclusiveness of contra-absolutist arguments without bringing in considerations that are "external" to the moral point of view itself.[20] Now historically, liberalism has not only permitted but depended upon external considerations of many kinds—for instance, religious considerations. But in common with most contemporary liberal theorists, Fishkin believes that a secular "neutrality" among external considerations of every kind is a prerequisite to avoiding tyranny—tyranny, for example, like that of Iran under the mullahs.[21]

The point is well taken, but one must wonder whether it has been misapplied. For as we have seen, neutrality over the question of *excellence of character* in those who are to *take* the moral point of view is itself an invitation to tyranny—no matter how "external" considerations of character may be. Alongside the Ayatollah Khomeini we should remember Adolph Eichmann.

Perfectionism

There is not much good in priming an engine unless it is already in good order, and in the same way there is not much good in priming the faculties of imagination, sympathy, and intellect unless they too are in good order. In other words, the priming principles will not dispose these faculties to interact in just the right way unless certain *pre*dispositions are already in place. The view that I will call "perfectionism" calls these *virtues* or, simply, excellences.

Certain things happen to the interpretation of the priming principles when we link them with the operation of the virtues. In the first place, besides the very general priming principles, we begin to think of a host of specialized priming principles, each of which activates a particular predisposition. Aristotle calls these the "principles of the virtues." In the second place—and more important—we begin to think of the general priming principles themselves differently than we did before. Liberals prefer maxims like "Put yourselves in the other's shoes" and construe this as meaning that one should be ready to put his or her own good *aside* for the good of others. Since this suggests that one's own good and the good of others are at odds, it inevitably raises a question that it cannot answer: why should one be moral? But from the perfectionist outlook, part of the point of speaking of "excellences" of character at all is to suggest that they are *good to have*. In the case of the social virtues, which prompt a regard for the good of others, the presumption is that one's own good *partially comprehends* the good of others. For instance, I am not setting my own good aside when I care for my children or my friends; if they languish, my own life is in some measure deficient; I "identify." Obviously there are limits to this identification. But whereas some liberals (and some other contra-

absolutists) prefer to think in terms of a sheer opposition between one's own good and the good of others which can be only
contingently overcome, perfectionists prefer to think in terms of
a persistent tension between a narrow and a comprehensive understanding of one's own good.

Aristotle makes the comprehensive character of one's own
good very clear when he treats two different descriptions of the
flourishing soul as virtually interchangeable: the first, that its
activity is "in accord with reason"—that is, marked by self-
understanding and purpose, as we have seen; the second, that its
activity is "in accord with virtue," including the social virtues.[22]
This does *not* mean any of the things that either David Hume or
his adversaries may have taken it to mean. Rather, the point is
that these two descriptions are virtually interchangeable because
we are *social beings:* we depend upon one another in order to
understand ourselves, and we cannot develop our characteristic
powers without having purposes in common.

A compatible view, though a much stronger one, is expressed
in the biblical command to "love thy neighbor as thyself," given
in the Book of Leviticus in the Old Testament and reaffirmed as
one of the two greatest commands by Jesus in the Gospels of
Matthew, Mark, and Luke.[23] "Love" is here to be understood as
a virtue rather than as an emotion, as the disposition that under-
lies the systematic will to someone's good. To love one's neighbor *as* one's self clearly implies that in systematically willing the
good of one's neighbor, one wholeheartedly continues the systematic will to one's own good as well. The reason I characterize
this view as much stronger than the Aristotelian view is that it
does demand that love be taken to the point of literal selflessness:
one must be willing to "lose" oneself. Yet the *outcome* is that one
somehow "saves" oneself. Love in this dimension is held to be
beyond the capacity of merely natural powers; it requires the
invasion of Nature by Grace. Consequently, to secularize the
concept (for instance, to turn it into "altruism") is to render it
unintelligible. Having been touched by this kind of love, I believe in it and further believe that it is more important than
anything else I speak about in this book; but I can speak competently of only one thing at a time, and I am too much a novice to
speak competently of *that* at all. Therefore, I hew to my original

intention of speaking in this book about the ground that secular and Christian naturalists have in common.

At any rate, if the sheer opposition between one's own good and the good of others turns out to be "only" a persistent tension between a narrow and a comprehensive understanding of one's own good, one may still ask whether the prospects are reasonable for resolving that tension in this world, and that is a perfectly respectable secular question. For that matter, one may ask whether we are very good at caring for our own good, even *aside* from its bearing on the good of others; I suspect that the medieval Christians knew what they were doing when they listed "acedia," or "sloth," an insufficient zeal for the good as such, as a particularly tempting sin.[24] Irrespective of how good for us the excellences may be, does anyone flawlessly achieve them?

Aristotle always writes as though he were absolutely assured of his own virtue, although he regards perfection as attainable only by philosophers. Plato, with perhaps more insight than his student Aristotle, admits through the main character in his *Republic* that philosophers are really rather more likely to become vicious than other men—especially, it seems, the ones who study morality.[25] Christianity simply declares that perfect virtue is a good beyond the reach of fallen man, and holds out the promise of redeeming Grace. Modern political theory, as we saw in the first chapter, began with flat statements that man is not only bad but irredeemably bad. No doubt the last position is extreme, but complete excellence is *at least* rare, and that creates a problem for the perfectionist strategy of justification which it cannot resolve on its own terms.

The problem may be simply stated. Perfectionism departs from contra-absolutism in regarding arrival at the *right* practical conclusions as dependent not only upon taking the "moral point of view" but also upon possessing the virtues. But if perfect virtue is rare, then the way in which we justify our practical conclusions to others cannot be patterned after the way in which we arrive at them beforehand after all. Besides having to invoke the "moral point of view," we are now put in the paradoxical, absurd, and hypocritical position of having to tell others how virtuous we are. This is *paradoxical* because constant arguments about who possesses virtue are themselves detrimental to virtue.

It is *absurd* because we can never convince the others that we do have virtue. And it is *hypocritical* because in all likelihood we don't have much anyway.

Lapsarianism

Although perfect virtue is at least rare and perhaps nonexistent, it by no means follows that we are perfectly depraved. If we were vicious through and through, if virtue were wholly alien to our character, it would also be wholly alien to our imagination. (There *are* people to whom virtue is totally invisible, and to whom its outward signs seem to betray an elaborate and mysterious con, but these, we hope, are few.) So from a limited purchase on virtue we gain a limited idea of what it is to flourish. This in turn gives us an idea what to "look for," so that we are sometimes (not always) able to recognize individuals whose characters exceed the common run.[26] By observing these individuals and extrapolating from what we see in them, we are able to hazard rough generalizations about the sorts of things that individuals with perfect virtue *would* or *would not* do under various circumstances. This is what I will call a "lapsarian" strategy.

Of course, these generalizations are flawed in the same way that all inductions and extrapolations are flawed, but they are nothing to sneeze at; in particular, they *supplement* our arguments from the "moral point of view" *without* requiring us to be certain of our own virtue or of the virtue of one another. They are, as it were, "privileged" general-purpose practical conclusions—applicable in a more nearly deductive way than the priming principles to a wide variety of circumstances—from which we should deviate only with the greatest caution and reluctance.

This makes them important in two ways. In the secret recesses of the soul, they serve as diagnostic instruments that assist us in cultivating the health of character we do not yet have. In the light of common day, they provide a prima facie basis for arguments of justification, a basis which, because it is grounded in an *idealization* of the way we tend to come to our practical conclusions, need not coincide with the way any particular individual actually *has* come to his practical conclusions. Because this is a satisfactory settlement of the question of how the way we arrive at our practical conclusions should be related to the way we justify them to others, it solves the problem of the rational unity of motive. The solution also has obvious bearing on the role of *models* of virtue from art and life in the moral education of the young.

One may ask whether the generalizations that the lapsarian strategy yields are the same as the "natural laws" that classical and early modern moral thinkers were always talking about. The question is worth discussion, although I would like to stress that its importance is very much secondary and "academic." Moreover, the answer to the question is "Yes and No," because classical and early modern thinkers called all sorts of things natural laws. For example, the two senses of the term that had the widest currency in early modern thought were (1) that natural laws are the laws of our innate dispositions, and (2) that natural laws are "theorems of prudence": the phrase is Hobbes's, and it means maxims that tell a man how to find his advantage in the world, given what he knows to be the innate dispositions of everyone else.[27] But neither of these two senses concerns us here.

In another, more classical sense of the term, natural laws are just priming principles. This seems to be what Thomas Aquinas has in mind when he gives the first principle of natural law as "Good ought to be ensued, and evil avoided,"[28] for obviously this stands in need of interpretation. The interpretations we make in the light of the virtues, he calls the secondary principles of natural law, and they too seem to function as priming principles. My reading of Thomas at this point is likely to be controversial because his tendency to characterize the *application* of the principles of natural law in syllogistic terms gives the impression that he is an absolutist. The view of Thomas as an absolutist cannot be maintained, however, because the minor term of a practical syllogism cannot be formulated without an exercise of judgment, and this exercise, for Thomas, presupposes the possession of the virtues.

There is another way of using the term "natural laws," one that I favor and that is classical in character, although I am unable to attribute it to any specific classical thinker. Things that are good for human beings always constrain the ways in which

93

they may be sought; the constraints are in their very nature. For instance, true friendship involves a moderate degree of self-disclosure. It follows that although I might be able to attract companions by misrepresenting myself, I could never attract friends. I can therefore say, "Never misrepresent yourself in pursuit of friendship." In view of certain tendencies in ordinary language philosophy, this may be misunderstood. The prevailing usage of the English words "friend" and "companion" is irrelevant here. Rather, the point is that a certain kind of relationship is a human good. If we did not have the word "friend" for it, or if that word referred to something else, we would have to make up a word for it; and if we did not have a word in the English language that functions like the word "companionship," so that we could distinguish the relationship denoted by this word from the one denoted by "friendship," we would have to make up a word for that relationship, too.[29] Natural laws may then be thought of as expressing the constraints that human goods impose upon the ways in which they may be pursued. They cannot be exhaustively enumerated, but the virtue traditionally called "wisdom" is in large part the ability to recognize them quickly, under a wide range of circumstances, coupled with the constant will to act within the constraints they express.[30] This is worth stressing, because the emphasis in Aristotle's discussion of wisdom is different.

Is this understanding of natural law inconsistent with a transcendentalist view of morality? Different, definitely, but not inconsistent. There may be transfinite multitudes of "true" laws of which the generalizations yielded by the lapsarian strategy are approximations. Such a correspondence would be unlikely, of course, unless our Nature had been deliberately designed by a boundless Intelligence in just such a fashion that the lapsarian strategy *would* yield such generalizations for us. It has been said that whenever Shakespeare deviates from the pale formulas that we call the "laws of poetry," the grace of the resulting lines vindicates him; he is following the true laws after all, but they defy formulation by human intellect. This is something like that.

The Fulfillment of Nature

Virtues, or excellences, are those dispositions which further a life of rational unity as discussed in Chapters Two and Three. In the Mezzalogue the operation of these dispositions is described in four dimensions, integral, intimate, practical, and political, setting the stage for Chapters Four and Five.

Excellence in General

Although there certainly are rules that human beings ought to follow, the thrust of the two preceding chapters is that our Nature achieves its fulfillment not so much in the following of rules as in the blossoming of *qualities*, which these rules imperfectly nourish and express. In this mezzalogue (I apologize for the neologism, but I haven't any other name for an in-between half-chapter), I would like to pause to say something about these qualities. So far I have used different names for them. The name "virtue" is a concession to common usage, but it has drawbacks. When Aristotle used the word that we translate as "virtue," the term *arete*, he meant a specific excellence that contributes to a person's being what we understand or should understand a human being to be, an inward means of his attention to his truest good. Unfortunately, the English word "virtue" suggests something more in the way of priggish regard for external observances, or even *dis*regard for one's truest good; for us, disregard for one's truest good has very nearly come to be regarded as the

proper subject of ethics, "altruists" that we say we are. Therefore, I will continue to use the word "excellence," as well as the
word "virtue," to denote a quality of a flourishing soul.

One point that was merely implicit in my previous discussion
requires elaboration here. As Aristotle observed, the excellences
are qualities involving *choice;*[1] to put the same thing another way,
they are above all dispositions of *will*. This means that they are
to be distinguished from passions on the one hand, and from
capacities on the other.[2] For instance, neither compassion (as the
name implies, a passion) nor intelligence (a capacity) is an excellence. Why this should be so is easy to see: misplaced compassion may tip the scales of justice, and misdirected intelligence
may lead me to plan the perfect crime. That these distinctions
are misunderstood in contemporary political culture is the worse
for us; praise of a politician *simply* for his or her compassion or
intelligence is always beside the point. Yet clearly, to *distinguish*
excellences from passions and capacities is not the same as to
claim that the former have nothing to do with the latter. If a man
is deficient in some passion or capacity, he is also likely to be
deficient in the excellences, because it will not be there when
excellence requires it. For instance, although practical wisdom is
not the same thing as intelligence, it does have need of intelligence; likewise, although mercy is not the same thing as compassion, it does call upon it. The point of complete excellence is
that each passion and capacity is to be called upon "at the right
time, toward the right objects, toward the right people, for the
right reason, and in the right manner" by a deeply seated disposition of character.[3] A consequence is that although passions
can be misplaced and capacities can be misdirected, "misplaced
virtue" is a contradiction in terms. Whenever we are tempted to
speak in this way, we have either misunderstood the virtue in
question or else taken something to be a virtue that is not a virtue
at all.

In calling the excellences "dispositions," we also have to distinguish between the well-*disposed* individual, and the merely
well-*controlled* individual. The first is the classical ideal, one who
experiences the passions fully but appropriately. By contrast,
the passions of the well-controlled individual are often likely to
be inappropriate to the occasion, but he knows this, and when

they become unruly he simply suppresses them.[4] In their emphases on rules and the censorship of impulses, outlooks as diverse as Calvinism, the psychoanalytic theory of personality, and most varieties of liberalism agree in taking the well-controlled rather than the well-disposed individual as the goal. In fact, from these perspectives, even to entertain the possibility of the well-disposed individual is nothing less than utopian. But this is a half-truth. It is true insofar as the classical ideal of the well-disposed individual is never *perfectly* realized. It is false insofar as it implies that conditions which are never perfectly realized are ineligible as ideals. If that were true, then the only condition ever worth idealizing would be the way things are already. Ideals are disqualified not when we cannot perfectly realize them but when we cannot even move toward them. For the next four sections of this chapter I will go ahead and be "utopian." Compromises between the actual and the ideal will be put off until the end.

The Dimensions of Excellence

Now that we have a general idea what kind of qualities the excellences are, *which* qualities actually are excellences? Even after the exclusion of passions and capacities from the list, an immense number of candidates might seem to remain. Classical writers tried to bring order to the profusion by means of various schemes of classification. A glance at the scheme espoused by Aristotle will help to reveal the limitations of this approach.

According to Aristotle, every action and emotion can be characterized in terms of its position along certain *ranges*, each of which is bounded by "excess" at one end and "deficiency" at the other.[5] For instance, there is a range of action and emotion bounded at one end by rashness and at the other by cowardice, and another bounded at one end by obsequiousness and at the other by grouchiness. Now what Aristotle calls a man of "wisdom" (*phronesis*) is a man whose deliberation about what to do is guided by a correct intuition of the relationship between partial goods and the comprehensive good. Such a man can always perceive the right place to be, along any of these ranges. This "right place to be" is what Aristotle calls the "mean," although this is not to be construed as the midpoint; in fact, just *where* along the range the mean falls depends upon circumstances and may even be different for different individuals. Clearly, wisdom is an excellence. But we can also speak of a set of narrower excellences, each of which is associated with just *one* of the ranges I have mentioned. What each of *these* excellences does is dispose the individual to observe the mean relative to the *particular* range with which it is associated. For instance, the excellence that disposes the individual to observe the mean relative to rashness and cowardice is simply *courage*,[6] while the excellence that disposes the individual to observe the mean relative to obsequiousness and grouchiness is simply *friendliness*.[7] These are the same means that *would* be recognized by the wise man, even though the courageous or friendly man is not necessarily wise too. Consequently, although wisdom tends to perfect the other excellences, they can be possessed imperfectly without it. Whether wisdom can be possessed without *them* is an open question.

This scheme is powerful and suggestive. Besides courage and friendliness, Aristotle is able to characterize eight other dispositions (nine, counting justice)[8] as means between excess and deficiency along some range or other. In loose paraphrase, they are ease in self-command, generosity, public-spirited munificence, a high-minded sense of one's own deserts, a moderate ambition for honors, gentleness, truthfulness, and wittiness.[9] But although these are all interesting candidates for designation as excellences, one is entitled to ask whether some of them might better characterize the urbanity of the Athenian man of rank than the flourishing of the soul. We could enshrine liberal democratic prejudices in the same way, and just as easily: we could characterize independence as a mean between eccentricity and conformity, for example, or industriousness as a mean between drivenness and laziness. Thus the first defect of the Aristotelian scheme is this: it is better able to *describe* dispositions than to establish that they are, in fact, excellences.

The second defect is even more serious. Many of the candidates for designation as excellences cannot be characterized in terms of excess and deficiency at all. This is obviously the case with wisdom, otherwise Aristotle's scheme would become circular: excellence would be defined in terms of the mean which an excellent man would observe. He again laid this scheme aside in his discussion of a second kind of wisdom, which he called "theoretical" by contrast with the first kind, which is "practical."[10] Or suppose we were to leave Aristotle and entertain the Christian hypotheses that the excellences include faith, hope, and love. Since all three are dispositions rather than passions or capacities, they are at least admissible as candidates. But between what excess and what deficiency is faith, for instance, the mean? One is tempted to say that the excess is "credulity" while the deficiency is "incredulity"—but in the first place those terms refer to dispositions of *belief*, which concerns cognition, whereas faith is a disposition of *surrender*, which concerns relationship; and in the second place, although the idea of surrender to God is presented along with an emphasis on the continuing distinctness and worth of the persons who make this surrender, the surrender is nevertheless utter and unconditional and cannot be conceived as a "mean."

Other classification schemes fail for similar reasons. I do not believe that any single classification scheme, or manageably small set of such schemes, can characterize all and only those qualities that really are excellences. Another drawback of insistence on particular schemes of classification is that it encourages the confusion of form with substance. For instance, although Plato discusses excellence of character under four headings while Aristotle discusses it under thirteen (or eleven with two left over),[11] who is to say that these enumerations do not cover the same ground?

In order to know whether different enumerations *do* cover the same ground, and to argue over stretches of ground that seem to be covered by some enumerations but not by others, we need a way to survey all the ground that *can* be covered without actually naming specific excellences. One such way presents itself in the fact that there is only a small number of "dimensions" in which the excellences operate, or manners in which they may contribute to a flourishing life. I describe the first four of these dimensions in the four short sections following. There is at least one more, but—as I indicate in the Epilogue—it is not wholly within the ken of natural philosophy.

Integral Excellence

One of the sayings whose meaning changed after the classical tradition was abandoned is that we are "naturally social." Moderns have generally taken this to mean either that we are innately gregarious or that (poorly equipped with claws, hair, forelegs, and so on) we depend upon each other for our survival—neither of which is necessarily true. In the classical tradition the saying meant that outside of society, we cannot develop either the excellences or the passions and capacities upon which the excellences draw. When in the eighteenth century a boy was found who appeared to have survived all alone in the French countryside since shortly after infancy, his inability to adapt to society—for that matter, his very survival—seemed to prove that we are not naturally social at all. But if the saying is taken in its original sense, of course the boy confirms it.

Now although none of the excellences can be cultivated outside of society, it by no means follows that none of them can be *described* without reference to society. Up to a point, we *can* talk about the qualities that further purposiveness and self-understanding, without elaborating their dependence upon other beings with whom purposes may be shared and to whom understandings may be disclosed. Simply because they describe a sort of wholeness or integrity, we may call these *integral* excellences. On a first pass at the problem, we may come up with candidates like resiliency, strength and constancy of will, courage on one's own behalf, self-respect joined with lack of pretense, and patience. These are plausible enough; all of them seem to further the development of purposes, the commitment to purposes, the transparency of purposes, the critique of purposes, and the realization of purposes (although realization of purposes also depends upon how one is situated in the world). But greater precision can be gained by asking which qualities of the soul support the resolution of the three "problems of rational unity" discussed in the last chapter. In fact, it appears that this is exactly what many writers in or near the classical tradition have done. For instance, Aristotle's exploration of the relationship between practical wisdom and the other excellences engages the problem of the rational unity of motive; the classification of excellences that Plato provides in his *Republic* engages the problem of the rational unity of character; and more recently, MacIntyre has resorted to a discussion of the problem of the rational unity of a whole life in order to explain why patience, constancy, and "integrity," in his own sense of the term, are excellences. These partial efforts, and others like them, may require little more than to be coordinated in terms of the total picture: the problem of rational unity taken in *all* of its aspects. Perhaps this could serve as the basis for debate over the integral excellences if we succeed in resurrecting Nature.

Intimate Excellence

Eventually we *do* reach the point where nothing more can be said without finally asking just how purposiveness and self-understanding depend on the opportunity to share purposes and understandings with others. The dimension of excellence that *enables* us to conceive and pursue purposes in common and that *sustains* mutual disclosure may be called "intimate." We aren't necessarily speaking of an entirely different set of qualities from those discussed before; for instance, the quality of self-respect joined with lack of pretense contributes to a certain transparency along both the integral and the intimate dimensions. Nor are we necessarily speaking of exactly the *same* set of qualities as before; for instance, we might now wish to consider courtesy, devotion, loyalty, complaisance (although not complacency), and that nameless quality that lies between frankness and reserve as candidates for designation as excellences. Often, when an intimate quality is recognized as a bona fide excellence, the act of recognition will force us to reinterpret integral excellences we have already considered. If we recognize complaisance as an intimate excellence, for example, then we have no choice but to distinguish strength and constancy of will from sheer stubborn selfishness—something we might not have done otherwise. Of course, this is not to say that departures from selfishness are "altruistic" or "disinterested." On the contrary, consideration for intimates is *intensely* interested, as I have already remarked. It is comprehended within our own good.

Just why purposiveness and self-understanding do depend on cooperation and self-disclosure is worth far more thought than it received in the classical tradition, and this may be one point at which naturalism can draw from modernity. Omitting theological explanations,[12] if the supposal is true that the rational unity of a whole life is the unity of a special kind of narrative in which the "self" is both author and main character, then one of the capacities upon which even integral excellence draws must be narrative competence, or linguistic competence generally; and if it is also true, as Wittgenstein claimed, that there can be no such thing as a "private language,"[13] then in at least one respect, intimate excellence is more nearly the prerequisite for integral excellence than the reverse. But this is only a schema for a possible explanation, not the explanation itself. The natural basis for the social development of linguistic competence is not even universally acknowledged, much less fully understood.

If excellence in a life depends partly upon being able to share it with others, so do some forms of pathology, and it must be a part of excellence to be immune. Simply because life is on view, one can easily lose the distinction between living and being viewed— can become an *actor* instead of a character, and shape the narrative around the felt needs of the spectator. The issue then becomes what one takes these needs to be.

One type of actor takes these needs to be tragic. Aristotle thought that one of the reasons for the performance of tragic drama is the opportunity it affords spectators to be purged of their fear and pity.[14] The *spectacle* of pain, in other words, can be cleansing, and to be cleansed in this way is a need. Now it is also true that in another sense, pain and grief can be cleansing for real subjects. However, the conditions that *make* pain a cleansing experience are quite different for the witness of an enacted spectacle and for a real subject. Thus losing the distinction between living and being viewed is more than unrealistic; it can be catastrophic, and the tragic mask can become fused with the face as a kind of rotten chrysalis. This is the fate of the character of Satan in Milton's *Paradise Lost*, who cuts a noble figure because he has lost interest in everything but the figure he cuts. But the spectacle of voluntary suffering is reenacted daily in smaller ways—in realms as diverse as marriage and existential theorizing.

Practical Excellence

Intimate excellence cannot long be discussed without distinguishing the *kinds* of intimate (or potentially intimate) relationships: marriage, friendship, parent with child, teacher with disciple, patron with client, and so forth. But the very act of distinguishing them discloses that they depend upon, and sustain, broader social contexts. A marriage, for instance, creates an economic unit. A friendship can seal trust between partners in business. The relationships of parent with child and of teacher with disciple reproduce a vision of how to live, which is (sometimes) a means by which society reproduces itself. Patron-client relationships confer legitimacy upon traditional elites by creating reciprocal obligations between members and nonmembers.

But in these broader contexts, purposes are often—even usually—shared without self-disclosure; obversely, even the purposes of intimates can be partly at odds. To be sure, we have laws to regulate our social conflicts. But even the efficacy of law presupposes certain qualities among the population, not to mention the law's administrators. Consequently we cannot long avoid discussing "practical" excellence: the excellence that sustains social practices and institutions.

Needless to say, not every quality that sustains a social practice or institution is an excellence, for some practices and institutions are inimical to human flourishing. The qualities that make a man a "good" assassin or pornographer, for instance, are not what I have in mind. But the institutional supports for the excellences elsewhere discussed depend in turn upon excellence in the sense under discussion now. For instance, the material security of my household, an economic unit, provides an institutional support to my marriage, a relationship of intimacy. The intimate excellences are needed to sustain my marriage, but the practical excellences are needed to sustain my household.

These practical excellences may include mundane qualities like diligence or reliability—and this creates a problem. The intimate excellences are, or easily become, their own reward. Practical excellences *can* also become intrinsically rewarding, but to bring this about is much more difficult. Now here is an oddity: from some points of view, the problem I have just introduced is invisible. That is worth a long digression.

One of the viewpoints from which the problem is invisible is Alasdair MacIntyre's. MacIntyre defines a social "practice" in an intricate way, as

> any coherent and complex form of socially cooperative human activity through which goods internal to that form of activity are realized in the course of trying to achieve those standards of excellence which are appropriate to, and partially definitive of, that form of activity, with the result that human powers to achieve excellence, and human conceptions of the ends and goods involved, are systematically extended.[15]

Here MacIntyre is not using the term "excellence" in my sense, as synonymous with "virtue"; rather he is speaking about excellent performance of an activity. On the other hand his passage *does* have to do with virtue in another way—in fact, with practical virtue—as will shortly become clear. Before we can talk about that we have to understand just what he is saying here.

The complexity of MacIntyre's definition results in part from his attempt to construct it in such a way as to avoid reliance upon the concept of Nature in everything that touches upon the virtues. Of course, since in claiming that we are "naturally social," the classical writers meant *no more* than that we are so made that we cannot systematically extend our powers and our conceptions of possible ends *except* through participation in the multiplicity of socially cooperative forms of human activity, one is bound to wonder just how this definition does banish Nature. But I will not linger on the point, because it is obvious and because other matters demand elucidation. The most important of these matters is the notion of goods being "internal to practices."

The notion is not quite original to MacIntyre. It seems to be closely related to a distinction introduced to the study of Aristotle by L. H. G. Greenwood in 1909[16] and more recently used by John M. Cooper to clarify the doctrine of virtue propounded by

Aristotle himself.[17] Greenwood was perplexed by what Aristotle meant when he spoke of "means to ends." The reasons why he found this cloudy in Aristotle's works do not concern us here, but in order to clear things up, Greenwood distinguished between (1) "external" or "productive" means, and (2) "constituent" or "component" means. The former are means in the sense familiar to speakers of English: they are causal conditions that must be satisfied before certain ends can be produced. For instance, if I don't strike a match, I won't get a fire. The latter are means in a different sense: they contribute to ends by being *parts* of what the ends are all about. Cooper convincingly argues (against Greenwood, it so happens) that Aristotle regarded the virtues not only as external but also as constituent means to the good life. This view correlates with a number of remarks already made in this book, most recently that the virtues are or can become intrinsically rewarding. However, it also correlates with MacIntyre's argument that the virtues are among the goods "internal to practices," an argument offered shortly after the definition quoted above.

Now according to MacIntyre, a good is "external to a practice" when it is attached to the practice only by "accidents of social circumstance." One of the practices of our society, for example, is tournament chess; and although the goods of prestige, status, and money are attached to it, they are only attached externally. In another society that happened to practice tournament chess, they might not be attached to it at all.[18] By contrast, the goods "internal" to the practice of chess are "the achievement of a certain highly particular kind of analytical skill, strategic imagination and competitive intensity"[19]—and these three goods, MacIntyre says, can be neither possessed, identified, nor recognized in any way *but* by actual participation in the practice. Here is the payoff: the qualities of character that *sustain* the pursuit of excellent performance as it is understood within a practice and that also sustain the kinds of *relationships* the practice involves are clearly *also* goods "internal" to the practice. *These qualities*, according to MacIntyre, give us our first rough cut at the virtues.

This approach is odd in at least three ways, the last of which will return me to the point at which I began this digression.

First, MacIntyre does not say that he is giving us a rough cut at the practical virtues; he says that he is giving us a rough cut at the virtues, *simply*. That his approach provides no basis for the integral virtues is not important, because he provides a different basis for them much later. It *is* important that his approach provides no foundation for the intimate virtues, except perhaps by construing all the forms of intimacy as just so many "practices." Although this is not fatal, it is very awkward and is probably symptomatic of the strain of trying to build a theory of the excellences without making reference to human nature. We would do better to confine his approach to the practical virtues.

Even so we are not out of hot water, for the approach is rather too open to the hypothesis that *all* social practices are good. This is the second oddity. MacIntyre does at least consider the possibility that there may be such a thing as an evil social practice,[20] but—misplacing the burden of proof—he adds that he is "far from convinced"; still, he rightly goes on to admit that for this reason (as well as the reason that even a *good* social practice may occasionally produce evil), social practices "stand in need of moral criticism," which can be provided only by examining their place "in some larger moral context." As he sees it, this "larger moral context" has an inner and an outer shell: the first is the lives of the individuals who engage in social practices; the second is the traditions in which these lives unfold. Both, says MacIntyre, must possess a kind of wholeness or unity—namely, narrative unity.

Having spent an entire chapter talking about the importance of narrative unity, I have no interest in denying this assertion. But *by itself*, doesn't it only push the problem of evil back a notch? The narrative unity of a life or of a tradition is only a necessary condition for its goodness, not a sufficient condition. Racist myths may have narrative unity; even the life of Satan in Milton's epic has narrative unity. Therefore, lives and traditions stand no less "in need of moral criticism" than do social practices, and this moral criticism can be provided only by examining their places in some *still* larger moral context. But because MacIntyre does not propose such an examination, one must suppose that he considers it unnecessary. This turns his theory into a relativism of virtues or, worse yet, a virtuous relativism.

My own response to the problem of regress in "larger moral

contexts" is twofold. First, narrative unity is not the only demand of our Nature; unity is also needed in the character of the
agent and among his motives for action. Second, even after these
natural demands have been satisfied, Nature herself is subject to
critique as but one of her Author's instruments. Down the first
part of this road, secular and Christian naturalists can travel
together. At the beginning of the second, of course, there is a
parting of the ways, and I will have more to say about this in the
Epilogue.

The third oddity of MacIntyre's approach is that it takes for
granted that *all* of the virtues relative to practices are "internal"
to them. Surely, though, qualities that *externally* sustain good
social practices ought to be counted as virtues, too—and this is
the point with which my digression on MacIntyre began. Something important can nevertheless be learned from his approach.
Noting his mistake helps to avoid the opposite mistake: without
his presentation it would have been easy to think that *all* of the
practical excellences are external to the activities they sustain.
This error would have been just as great, and that is an insight
for which he deserves grateful acknowledgement. Let me intro-
duce a distinction of terminology, between

1   practices in MacIntyre's sense and
2   institutions, conceived for present purposes as instrumen-
    tal in orientation and falling into two groups:
    a   those by which we reproduce and transform the *mate-
        rial conditions* of our common life, and
    b   those by which we reproduce and transform the *pattern*
        of that common life.

Then practical virtues may be *internal* to practices, and *external*
to institutions.

Political Excellence

Despite the brevity of this discussion, the compounding of the
"dimensions" of excellence is already beginning to assume siz-
able proportions. The family, for instance, is in its economic
aspects an institution by which we reproduce and transform the

material conditions of our common life, and in its educational aspects an institution by which we reproduce and transform the pattern of that common life. But in some societies it is also a chrysalis for intimate relationships and may even be organized around them. Moreover, in its educational aspects it can even double as a practice. This complexity is not unique to the family. All that we do, we do in many dimensions at once.

The family is like other institutions in another way, too: it operates on a small scale. Of course, the scale may vary; clans operate on a much larger scale than nuclear families. But in any community larger than a village, the scale on which the family operates is small compared with the community itself. One class of institutions offers a general exception to the rule of scale, and that is—by definition—the class of *political* institutions. Their operation is architectonic, not only because they order certain aspects of the overall life of the community (for in some communities they order very few) but also in that they confer the authority of the community upon such arrangements as enjoy that authority (even if these arrangements were achieved by other than political means). Whatever does this is political in at least one important sense.

In most other ways, the differences between political institutions and others are accidental rather than necessary. Like the family, political institutions can be chrysalises for intimate relationships, the relationship of patron and client, for instance. This is not to say that patron-client relationships are always harmonious, but neither are parent-child or husband-wife relationships. Also like the family, political institutions can be organized *around* these intimate relationships, as they have been in regimes as diverse as the Roman Republic and big city "machines." Finally, like the family, political institutions can also double as practices. When the family is merely an institution, raising children is likely to be no more than a way to obtain labor; when it doubles as a practice, raising children is also seen as intrinsically rewarding. Politics displays the same duality. The ends for the sake of which a fellow becomes political may be of a sort that we can define without reference to the political means he employs. He may want anything from full employment, to jobs for his friends. However, his ends may also be *internal* to politics. He may have a vocation for statesmanship. The way we view the political qualities will be different in each of these cases. In the first case they will be understood as just those qualities that suit a man for going after what he wants and eventually getting it. In the second they will be understood as qualities through the exercise of which our conceptions of the ends we might pursue in common are extended or refined.

In fact, this is one of the two points that most sharply divide classical and modern political theory. Modern writers tend to regard politics as a set of institutions and nothing more. Classical writers regarded it as a set of institutions doubling as practices. In fact, they went even further. Most practices are related to human flourishing only contingently. Tournament chess is exciting, for instance, but we can pass it up without compromising our potential as human beings. *Politics*, by contrast, is related to human flourishing essentially. A man who is not a citizen is still a man, but he is less than a man should be. However distant and formal our relationships with people with whom we are neither intimately nor practically involved, it is not precisely correct to say that we look upon them as we might look upon our physical surroundings—as means to our ends, and nothing more; or at any rate, when we do, we are never quite at ease. Even the most jaded denizens of bloated metropolises take a not altogether perverse pride in their collective cynicism. It is a sort of oblique recognition that we conceive our purposes and pursue our aspirations within horizons that are a little broader than our intimate and practical circles; even that we somehow *need* these more expansive horizons in order to reach an understanding of "who we are." As it becomes less oblique, this recognition culminates in a concern for the integrity of these horizons and the safety of the things they contain.

That is how I take the Aristotelian saying that "man is a political animal." Even so, I should distinguish two forms of the proposition. The weak form is that human beings cannot develop fully and properly unless they care in some way for the common good as well as for their own affairs, and along with this that they faithfully discharge their responsibilities as citizens. The strong form is that political "activism" is the only admissible form of political practice and the very substance of the good life.

I affirm the weak form. This is the mean along a range bounded at one end by the Lockean rejection of both forms and at the other by the Ciceronian embrace of the strong form. Locke thought that even in a state of anarchy, the moral understanding is complete and the moral personality lacks nothing, so that the only reason we quit this state is the "inconvenience" of being subject to one another's passions. So highly was activism honored in Cicero's *milieu* that when he depicted heaven as the place where great statesmen and generals went to their reward, his compatriots thought it very fine. Far be it from me to deny the importance of activism for those who are suited to it (or who benefit from it), but we should not pretend that it suits everyone; activism is a vocation. Political theory may give it a certain pride of place, but it is not the only practice that can lift one out of private concerns into the domain of the common good. No doubt the best forms of care for the common good vary a great deal from regime to regime; to liberal democracies, for instance, Alexis de Tocqueville thought associational activity particularly well suited.[21] We need not fit every regime into the same mold. However, we should be leery of those that *discourage* any of the forms of political practice—right on up to and including political activism.

The other point over which classical and modern political theorists duel is closely related to the first. Whether or not they regard politics as a possible set of practices, they clearly agree that *before* being a set of practices, politics is a set of institutions. The question then becomes, what kind of institutions are these? Are they only institutions of the kind that reproduce and transform the material conditions of our common life, or are they also institutions of the kind that reproduce and transform the pattern of that common life? Modern writers have tended to reply, the former; classical writers, the latter. In the modern view the furthest call of politics is to prosperity, order, and growth. In the classical view the furthest call of politics is that the excellences should flourish. Thomas Aquinas went so far as to say that the purpose of law is to "make men good."[22]

On the face of it, this maxim demands continuous intrusions into private life and the wholesale violation of individual autonomy. But Thomas himself meant little more by it than that criminals should be punished and that good men should be recognized. He went out of his way to say that human law should undertake neither to repress every vice (because under such a burden, imperfect men would "break out into yet greater evils")[23] nor to prescribe every act of virtue (because even though no virtue is wholly unconnected with the common good, the same does not hold for every *act* of virtue).[24] Thus he explains that "the purpose of law is to lead men to virtue, not suddenly, but gradually."[25]

Perhaps this is too sanguine. What about the Greek thinkers? To Plato and Aristotle (whom we like to lambast for failing to distinguish between "state" and "civil society"), the whole of public life is an education, whether or not we will it, whether or not we even know it. So far as they are concerned, there is no such thing as a major social practice or institution that has no effect on character. As pearls and tumors form in the viscera of an oyster, so our temperaments are formed in the viscera of society—subtly, by degrees, perhaps even contrary to intentions, but inevitably. This is a disturbing reflection. It is very convenient to tell concerned liberals that to let ourselves be shaped by practices and institutions, without first shaping them to suit our possibilities, is the greatest danger imaginable to that "individual autonomy" they prize so greatly. But they may well ask in reply: Should we shape without scruple? In order to protect our "autonomy," must we embrace the Total State? Cruel paradox!

One might venture the flip reply, "Only a modern could entertain such a fantasy," and there would even be something to it. With Marx, we children of the Enlightenment believe that mankind always sets for itself only such problems as it can solve, and we suffer the further delusion that reasonable men and women have always thought so. Seeing that the classical writers perceived a political problem, we take it for granted that (as *we* would) they must have conceived a political solution. But they were not burdened with our optimism. From the claim that the furthest call of the political man is to promote the institutional conditions under which the excellences are most apt to flourish, it does not follow that he must imagine either his art or his wisdom to be wholly equal to the task. Why not? Because institutionalized, radical intrusion into social practices and institutions would have to be put in the scales just like the social practices and institutions that it would penetrate. Intrusion is also a social practice; it too would shape us even beyond what was intended by its planners. And from the experience of totalitarian regimes, we know what shapes it makes of men and women, and we reject them. Shall we then shape without scruple? One might just as well try to increase the population by legalizing rape (something that is not unprecedented, incidentally, as any good student of Roman history knows). The *true* political man approaches social practices and institutions more in the manner of a lover, whose audacity is tempered by courtly restraint.

Although I believe everything that I have just said, I hardly expect it to be convincing: the issue is too serious and complicated to be waved aside. I deal with it at greater length in the next two chapters, the first of which attempts to *allay* the fears of liberals, while the second attempts to redirect them.

The Desperation of Excellence

Dante Alighieri called this world a "threshing floor," an image that ought to give us pause. However true it is that in order to thrive, humans beings must conceive and pursue purposes and understandings in common, most of our energy goes into thwarting one another. Not only do individuals pursue solitary aims heedless of the common good, but the purposes shared within different communities may set them in implacable opposition. Perhaps in a world in which the virtues were perfectly developed, there would be none but trivial conflicts, but that is not the world of our concern. Here, our virtues are barely developed at all. This confronts us with the paradoxical necessity to rethink what perfect virtue *would* be if we *could* find it, because placed in this torn world, a perfectly virtuous individual would also have to be able to deal with its torn condition. This might be called the "desperation" of virtue. When to fight? When to subdue? When to submit? When to withdraw? When to turn the other cheek, and when to turn the moneychangers out of the temple with a whip? When to compromise, and on what terms?

If only the answers to these questions could be rendered in absolutistic formulae! They can't, although new priming principles, open ended like all priming principles, present themselves for consideration. "Compromise your demands," we may suggest, "whenever failure to do so would be destructive to the good for the sake of which those demands are made; but when compromise itself presents the greatest hazard to that good, forbear." Again, "Be willing to withdraw the demand for a secondary good for the sake of the comprehensive good that it is meant to further." At all costs, however, the seductions of casuistry must be avoided. The crucial thing to keep in mind is that these principles are meant only to trigger dispositions of character whose complete operation cannot be reduced to principles.

Thus now is the time to add *these* dispositions to the list of virtue candidates we have already compiled. What we are looking for are the "desperate virtues." The desperation of the human condition is the whole point of courage and resolution, for instance; and other qualities, like practical wisdom, certainly have desperate occasions.

This is not only an affair of the intimate, practical, and political dimensions of excellence. The desperation of excellence has ramifications in every dimension, including the integral. At the beginning of this Mezzalogue I drew a distinction between the well-controlled individual and the well-disposed individual, and said that virtue in the strict sense belongs only to the latter. That is true enough. By itself, though, it is misleading and stands in need of qualification. The fact is that we achieve self-control as a way station on the road to *becoming* well disposed. For this reason, there is both room and need to say something about what might be called "proto-virtues." Although proto-virtues may operate in any dimension, they are always simultaneously active in the integral dimension, coping with integral conflict.

These dispositions are familiar to all of us. They involve settled ways of calling upon the impulses Plato called "spirited"— shame, self-indignation, the sense of honor, and so on—in order to *make war* upon inappropriate impulses and *encourage* appropriate impulses. This is a difficult discipline, the fruit of which is virtue full and ripe. Temperance, for example, is not a mature virtue but the proto-virtue the mature analogue of which is moderation; likewise, bravery is the proto-virtue the mature analogue of which is courage. On the way from proto-virtues to mature virtues, from self-control to self-command, we may expect to witness greater and greater ease in bearing, greater and greater powers to discriminate among situations, and less and less tendency to use the priming principles, crutchlike, as though they were absolutistic axioms. However, since even the well-disposed individual may face integral conflict when sorely tried, the proto-virtues are not simply abandoned when true virtue begins to take hold. Rather they are held in reserve.

Despite the importance of holding the proto-virtues in reserve, however, they should never be confused with mature virtues. The goal is self-command without repression. On the way to that goal, repression has its uses, but it is very costly. What is merely repressed does not ordinarily disappear. Cut off its head and it hides. Hydralike, it grows three new heads in place of the old and returns in greater strength another day. The sooner appropriate exercises can be found for the impulses whose inappropriate expressions are repressed, the better. To everything its season, and a time for every matter under heaven; and when the times and seasons become woven into the fabric of our characters, the mechanisms of repression can be allowed to fade into the background.

Are courage, resolution, and the other desperate virtues intrinsically worthwhile, or is their worth due only to the circumstance of our living in a desperate world? So long as the world remains desperate, this question has no conceivable bearing on moral practice—and that is a good thing, because its answer is by no means clear. Conceivably, the character of the good can be illuminated all the more brilliantly by contemplating the possibility of its absence, a possibility that the desperate virtues presuppose. In his great poem, Dante had to pass through hell and purgatory to get from earth to heaven. Of course, he started from the very edge of despair; perhaps only in a desperate world is our understanding so darkened as to require such strenuous means of illumination. Then again, by another argument, good can be possessed only by choice, and choice requires awareness of the alternatives—something desperate virtues presuppose.

If there are any secular discussions of this question, they are

THE FULFILLMENT OF NATURE

unknown to me. The British philosopher P. T. Geach suggests that virtues of the kind I have called desperate are indeed intrinsically worthwhile and that God permits evil at least in part for the reason that these virtues would otherwise have no occasion to develop. Geach mentions courage in particular.[26] Arguments like this go back to Irenaus and Origen, and perhaps they are right. Perhaps God does know how to put evil to good uses. But we don't; therefore to imagine that we can discern His intentions in such matters is a risky business. According to ecclesiastical tradition, Origen's arguments were rejected in the early councils of the Church, and I suspect that this was the reason.

At any rate, the desperate virtues loom much larger in everyday life than the ordinary virtues—larger in every dimension. All of the considerations taken up in this section are highly pertinent to the remarks on compromise offered in the last chapter of this book.

CHAPTER FOUR

Nature Writ Large

Following up the discussion of the virtues in the Mezzalogue, Chapter 4 is about the *politics* of virtues, a term with twofold meaning: first, an approach to political evaluation that gives first place to considerations of excellence of character and how it may be cultivated; second, a set of practices and institutions in which this approach is or may be embodied.

The Politics of Virtues

Ancient moral theory gave first place to considerations of *virtues,* or excellence of character; by contrast, modern moral theory tends to give first place to considerations of *principles*, or rules that prescribe and justify conduct. As I showed in Chapter 3, a morality of virtues is not unprincipled any more than a morality of principles is vicious—each gives an account of principles, as well as virtues—but they give different solutions to the chicken-and-egg problem. Now the attempt to resurrect Nature has suggested that perhaps the morality of virtues ought to be brought out of the tomb along with it. But the ancients also insisted that politics founders without an ethical anchor, as we saw in the Mezzalogue.[1] Therefore, if we intend to take the morality of virtues seriously, shouldn't we also begin to take the *politics* of virtues seriously?

John Rawls regards the outlook that gives first place to considerations of excellence of character as a threat to the liberal ideals of liberty and equality.[2] But—aside from the fact that no ideals should be regarded as immune from scrutiny, even liberty and equality—we should not prejudge the issue of whether the morality and politics of virtues do or do not threaten the ideals we already hold. That archetypical liberal John Stuart Mill argued, in *Considerations on Representative Government*, that any set of political institutions should be judged under two heads: first, what it does to develop good qualities in the citizens, and second, what it does to organize the good qualities already existing in order to carry out the public business.[3] Startling as this may seem, coming from the pen of a utilitarian and former acolyte of Jeremy Bentham, it is hard to know what to call it if not a plea for a politics of virtues.

Now three things would be necessary for the implementation of a politics of virtues. The first would be a grasp of just what excellence of character really is. The second would be a grasp of how the concern for excellence relates to institutional design. The third would be a grasp of how the concern for excellence can be expressed in social policies. Of these issues, the first is perhaps most easily available to intuition but most difficult to spell out in theory. So, although I have tried to get a start on it in the preceding chapters, for present purposes I will be like the legendary economist alone on a desert island with a hundred cans of beans who "assumes a can opener" whenever he has the need. About the third issue, I do not think it would be wise to say much here at all. One who believes that all the circumstantial judgments necessary to frame good policy can be reduced to a few a priori maxims should busy himself with the morality and politics of principles, not the morality and politics of virtues. Therefore, I focus on the second issue. The next section seeks an overall perspective on institutional design. After it come three sections devoted to special problems, and the final section wraps up the discussion.

Excellence and Institutions

John Rawls—if I may be permitted to quote him again so soon—has complained that "so far, at least, there does not exist a

theory of just constitutions as procedures leading to just legislation."4

As stated, this remark is true. However, it would be false to
say that there is no tradition aiming to *produce* such a theory. In
fact, there have been several. Under any form of constitution,
the aspirations and motives of the citizens are channeled by political institutions so as to produce particular kinds of outcomes.
Theories differ according to what kinds of aspirations and
motives are reckoned with, according to how the process of
channeling is conceived, and according to what counts as a good
outcome. The theoretical outlook most encouraging to the morality of virtues—an outlook common in large measure to both
Aristotle and Mill—can be represented as shown in Diagram 1.
The solid arrows serve to call attention to the channeling process
already mentioned. Mill called this the "mechanical" side of government. What he called the "educational" side is represented

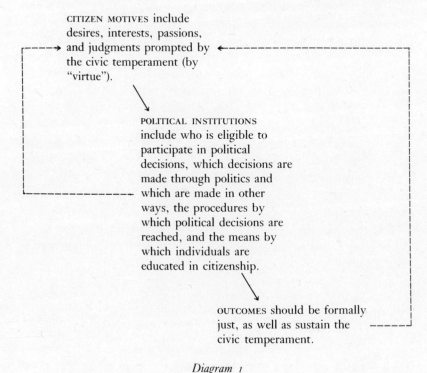

CITIZEN MOTIVES include
desires, interests, passions,
and judgments prompted by
the civic temperament (by
"virtue").

POLITICAL INSTITUTIONS
include who is eligible to
participate in political
decisions, which decisions are
made through politics and
which are made in other
ways, the procedures by
which political decisions are
reached, and the means by
which individuals are
educated in citizenship.

OUTCOMES should be formally
just, as well as sustain the
civic temperament.

Diagram 1

here by the dashed arrows; we may think of it as a sort of "feedback."[5] This is particularly important. Theorists in the tradition I am describing held that the aspirations and motives of the citizens are shaped not only by formal education and by the "natural lottery" of birth and class but also—deeply—by involvement or exclusion from political decisions, as well as by how the shoe pinches when these decisions are implemented. Mill also argued that although the features political institutions must have in order to be mechanically efficient do not vary much from culture to culture, the features they must have in order to nourish excellence among the citizenry vary a great deal.[6] Consequently the constitutional theorist is obliged to devote a much larger share of his thought to the educational than to the mechanical side of government.

Probably the kind of constitutional theorizing in *sharpest contrast* to the tradition just described is the kind that can be witnessed in modern "social-choice theory," although a close second could be found in the "neutralist" school of liberal ethics and jurisprudence.[7] The outlook of almost all contributors to social-choice theory can be represented as shown in Diagram 2.

CITIZEN MOTIVES are uniformly
characterized in terms of
orderings of preferences of
different individuals for
alternative states of affairs.

POLITICAL INSTITUTIONS are
conceived as embodiments of
rules by which individual
preference orderings are
"amalgamated" into "social"
preference orderings.

OUTCOMES should satisfy as
many citizens as possible
without violating any
principles of justice.

Diagram 2

Right away the eye is caught by the fact that the feedback arrows are missing; in other words, the educational side of government has dropped out of the picture, and only the mechanical side is left. A moment's reflection on what has happened to the description of citizen motives, political institutions, and outcomes shows why this was inevitable. In the first place, when we characterize all citizen motives in terms of individual preference orderings, we lose the power to distinguish between desires, interests, passions, judgments, and other sources of preference. A preference is a preference whether it is deeply seated in character or merely a garment of whim; whether it may yield to rational persuasion, to irrational persuasion, or to nothing at all. The information we need in order to talk about the cultivation of character is simply no longer available. In the second place, regarding political institutions *solely* as means by which preferences are "amalgamated" implies *refusing* to regard them also as means by which preferences are transformed through confrontation and discussion. To our other inabilities we may now add the inability to distinguish the social choice whether to go to war from the social choice whether to serve tea or coffee at the Congressional Prayer Breakfast.

In the third place—well, although the social-choice theorist speaks of satisfying as many individuals as possible while the member of the older tradition speaks of sustaining the civic temperament, at first glance it looks as though at least they meet each other halfway, for both speak of justice. But first glance is misleading, because what the social-choice theorist means by "justice" is very different from what the member of the older tradition probably means by it. The social-choice theorist is largely concerned with criteria against which the "fairness" of the preference amalgamation rule can be judged. These criteria are completely formal. For instance, the rule of amalgamating individual preference orderings by means of simple majority vote in successive pairwise comparison of the alternatives is blind in two different ways: blind to the differences among the alternatives, and blind to the identities of the individuals who are choosing among them. The social-choice theorist regards this as a good thing. In his language, the rule satisfies the "neutrality" and "anonymity" criteria (among others).[8]

By contrast, what Aristotle meant by justice has nothing to do with the amalgamation of preferences. Rather, justice is giving each individual what he merits; what he merits depends on the significance of his contribution to the life of the community; and the most significant contribution it is possible for him to make is to exercise practical wisdom during community deliberations. So, whereas for the social-choice theorist justice *precludes* the recognition of excellence (since that would violate the anonymity criterion), for anyone who agrees with Aristotle, justice *requires* the recognition of excellence (anonymity be damned). In fact, from his point of view, saying that outcomes should be formally just *as well as* sustain the civic temperament is simply redundant. Justice is integral with the educational side of government, and disregarding it amounts to disregarding the means by which the community makes itself possible.

By shifting the focus from Mill to Aristotle, I have neared the point—I may already have reached it—where liberals become alarmed. This concept of justice had better be examined more closely.

Excellence and Justice

Once again I will proceed by means of a contrast, this time a less drastic contrast than with social-choice theory. By and large, even neutralist liberals recognize such a thing as civic excellence, although they give it much less attention than another generation of liberals might have done (for instance, the generation including John Locke or the one including Adam Smith, both of whom come in for some attention later in the book). The reason why, despite this, many of them are sympathetic to the more procrustean outlook of mainstream social-choice theorists is that they conceive the *relation* between justice and the excellences in such a way that the problems of implementing a politics of virtues do not really arise.

For the sake of a brisk exposition, I will permit myself a great simplification. The general principles of justice are widely agreed among modern liberals to come before any other considerations in politics. Moreover, they widely agree that these principles apply not only to the formation of policy but also to the content of policy; in this, they part ways with social-choice theorists. However, they formulate the principles of justice at a very high order of abstraction. In order to be applied, these principles must be brought down to earth; they require further specification. This can be achieved only when they are combined with a due regard for economic circumstances. Thus the concrete (or detailed, or secondary) principles of justice—the ones that emerge from this due regard—will vary somewhat from community to community. Ideal circumstances would permit the formulation of concrete principles that *fully* realize the abstract principles of justice. Normal circumstances permit only a partial realization of the abstract in the concrete. So far, so good, but nothing yet has been said about civic virtue. It comes only at the very end of this explanation because for modern liberals it is a derivative idea. Essentially, it is nothing more than *conscientiousness*—the disposition to *abide* by the concrete principles of justice, whatever they turn out to be.[9] Therefore, it can be exhaustively characterized simply by listing these principles.

As just described, the logical structure of contemporary liberal theory looks like Diagram 3. Here the arrows represent the order of precedence among ideas, rather than the sequence of events and influences in the political regime itself:

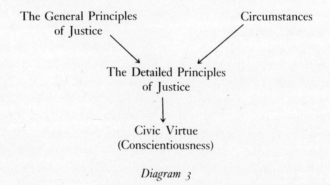

Diagram 3

A proponent of the politics of virtues would find three defects in this scheme, each of which he might well regard as fatal to it. First of all, it does not seem to tell us why anyone should *care* about being conscientious. "But aren't we entitled to assume that individuals are already willing to take a moral point of view? Why else would they listen to the moral theorist?" The proponent of the politics of virtues replies that this is just the problem: they may *not* listen. Worse, if "the moral point of view" is merely one of the less attractive among many points of view, there is no particular reason why they should. In this way of thinking, adequate moral theory does not concern itself so much with the "moral" point of view as with the *comprehensive* point of view, which, just because it is comprehensive, is moral. And it does not so much *exhort* us to take this view as it prepares us to *recognize* it. Ideally, we are already predisposed to take it because of the way we have been raised. Theory comes afterward, *vindicating* the way we have been raised (provided that it was the right way), and deepening and broadening the foundation then laid. Once we recognize the comprehensive view of the common good, we will discover that our excellences are the main constituents of that good; in fact, this is what makes them good. The awful conditionality of modern liberalism—"*if* (from some eccentricity) we take the moral point of view"—will ever be its downfall.

Second, it is unrealistic to believe that civic excellence can be exhaustively characterized simply by listing the concrete principles of justice. On the contrary, excellence is more like a fitness for seeing what those principles are. It has to come *before* them before it can come after them: the rules we teach children in order to shape their temperaments are much cruder than the ones they will follow in later life. Besides this, the liberal scheme tells us nothing about any dimensions of excellence other than the civic dimension—about wholeness of personality, concern for intimates, practical aptitude, or what have you. From this omission, one of two things may be inferred: that the civic dimension of excellence does not interact with the others at all, or that the other dimensions of excellence are wholly subordinate to the civic. Totalitarians embrace the second alternative; liberals, the first. But this, says the proponent of the politics of virtues, is as much as to say that the man who is desperately neurotic, indifferent to his friends, and wholly devoid of practical aptitude may yet be the very life and soul of the community—which is preposterous. To be fit to live in the City, a man or woman must be fit in a number of other ways as well. From the fact that the totalitarian errs, it does not follow that there is no error in the opposite direction.

The third objection takes up where the first leaves off. In the liberal scheme, where do abstract principles of justice come from in the first place? No one is quite certain. Some say that we are led to them by universally held intuitions or the modifications thereof; John Rawls has built on this idea in interesting and sophisticated ways.[10] But not everyone's intuitions are reliable, and the intuitions of some of us are even less reliable than those of others. Moreover, the more widespread that defects of character are, the more ludicrous it is to take the universality of an intuition as a testament to its reliability. Finally, although we may have no alternative but to depend on our intuitions at some point, what point is that? For it is by no means self-evident that the place to begin, in figuring out the principles of justice, is our intuitions about justice. Considering the high order of abstraction of the principles of justice, and their distance from interior experience, it is downright dubious. Justice may be a rather late derivative of something else, something that has greater immediacy—like what it is to thrive or flourish in a distinctively human way. In this case we should begin with our intuitions about that.

Although Aristotle's understanding of the relation between justice and virtue is also flawed, at least it is free of the flaws enumerated above. According to Aristotle, what is by Nature good for human beings comes before any other considerations in politics. Above all, this is a certain condition and activity of the soul marked by rational purpose and self-understanding.[11] Taken together, the excellences are just those dispositions that support this condition and sustain this activity. However, in order to *realize* our purposes, we need certain partial or qualified goods— goods that are not good in every context or in every measure or for every purpose; goods that people variously take to include wealth, honor, and political office, among others. But this raises distributive questions. Generally speaking, good institutions are those that support the human good—institutions, therefore, that cultivate and reward the excellences—and this is a concern of justice in the broadest sense. In the narrower sense, however, we call institutions just when they *distribute the things* that both the virtuous and the vicious desire (in their different ways) in such a fashion as to support the human good. Because our virtues prompt us to identify our own good in part with the good of the community, we care that justice in this sense should prevail.

Under ideal circumstances, Aristotle thought that we should give preeminence in the distribution of partial goods to the virtuous;[12] in so doing we would not only reward excellence in itself but also give political power to those to whom it is most safely entrusted. Under most circumstances, however, this is impossible. Virtuous citizens may be in short supply. Even if they are not, the claims of excellence must compete with various other claims: for instance, with the claims of the wealthy, who confuse merit with wealth; and with the claims of those who are not wealthy, who see merit in numerical superiority. As a practical matter, the claims of excellence cannot achieve victory under such circumstances, and it is a part of excellence to recognize the fact. At that, it would not be entirely fitting if they *could* achieve victory, for the community does need numbers, and it does need wealth (as well as individuals who can manage wealth for public ends). However, what the virtuous *can* do is try to *moderate* the various claims made in the community—including, among others, the claims of virtue per se, the claims of wealth, and the claims of numbers—and strike a balance among them.[13] Not every balance is a good balance, and mere stability does not make a balance good; a good balance is one that promotes the human good as fully as possible under the circumstances. If this balance is not administered by the virtuous themselves—as most of the time it will not be—then it must be administered under institutions that "imitate" excellence. These are institutions that foster outcomes as near as possible to those with which the excellent would concur. Although the balance achieved will quite properly vary with circumstances, it may be called "naturally" just, provided that the regard which circumstances receive is determined by the goal of furthering our unvarying natural good.

As I have described it, the structure of Aristotelian theory is shown in Diagram 4.

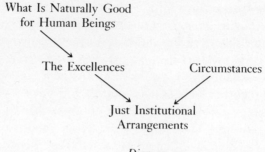

What Is Naturally Good
for Human Beings

The Excellences   Circumstances

Just Institutional
Arrangements

Diagram 4

What about this scheme? In the first place, some advocates of the morality of virtues—Alasdair MacIntyre, for one—are uncomfortable with Aristotle's naturalism.[14] I am willing to grant Aristotle's naturalism to him, of course. As I have explained earlier in this book, the attempt to ground an account of human excellence in something other than a teleological account of human nature leads even so competent a thinker as MacIntyre into circularities, as when he tries to say that "the good life for man is the life spent in seeking the good life for man," or that "a living tradition," in which individual quests for the good life may be embedded, is an argument "precisely in part about the goods which constitute that tradition."[15] Even so, Aristotle's use of the morality of virtues in his account of the politics of virtues cannot be accepted exactly as it stands.

One major defect is that Aristotle should have treated the excellences as he treated the rules of justice. Just as our unchanging natural good authorizes different institutional arrangements as "just" depending upon circumstances, *so it must authorize different versions of the excellences as appropriate* depending upon circumstances. Now this is a point where I am likely to be misunderstood. I am not proposing a marshy relativism or historicism, nor am I suggesting the subordination of the comprehensive human good to whatever promotes stability in each different kind of regime. To say that the appropriate application of an *unvarying* vision of excellence must vary somewhat according to the political culture under consideration is not to say that whatever is *considered* excellent in that political culture really is. My point is simply that the dispositions which most nearly sustain rational purpose and self-understanding under one set of circumstances and the dispositions which most nearly sustain it under another may differ in secondary respects. Although the body of moral truth is everywhere the same, it may change its clothing and vary its posture from time and place to time and place.

In order to explain this I think I had better leave the ivory tower for a moment. A Tanzanian missionary, Father Vincent J. Donovan, has written of his efforts to get loose from Western prejudices:

> With these Africans the purpose of words is not to establish logical truths, but to set up social relationships with others. That is quite a difference in the use of words.
>
> As an example, if I were in charge of a boarding school in East Africa and saw a boy break a window in the school, there are two ways I could deal with the situation.
>
> I could act out of my own Western culture and call him in and ask, "Johnny, did you break that window?" I want logical truth. He undoubtedly would say, "No," not because he is a liar, but because he is trying, with his words, to repair the social damage I have done with mine.
>
> The second way of dealing with the situation would be to act in consonance with his culture. I could call him in and say,
>
> "Hello, Johnny, how are you?"
>
> "Fine."
>
> "How are you doing in your studies?"
>
> "Better. I'm getting much better marks in math."
>
> "Good, how is your health?"
>
> "Not bad. The food here is good. I'm getting big and strong. I can now kick a football fifty yards. I kicked it through a window."[16]

If we agree with Donovan that the boy in this story is honest, then clearly there is something wrong with the idea that honesty is the disposition to speak nothing but logical truth. Yet the idea that words are to be used to establish social relationships is an incomplete substitute. There may be irresponsible as well as responsible social relationships. The boy is honest because he used his words to establish a *responsible* rather than an irresponsible social relationship. He did own up to his deed. And if honesty is the use of words to establish *only responsible* social relationships, then the selfsame virtue of honesty seems to be honored in both cultures, although the Western practice of that virtue is more closely bound up with the preservation of logical truth than is the East African practice. In cultural context, this difference may be entirely permissible. All the same, *both* practices may be criticized. *In the Western context*, would true human flourishing be better served by a looser association between the practice of honesty and the preservation of logical truth than that to which we now aspire? Likewise, *in the East African context*, would true human flourishing be better served by a *closer* relationship between them?

Here is a different kind of reflection on the relation between culture, and the interpretation of the excellences. Earlier I remarked that besides a civic dimension, excellence has an intimate dimension. I also mentioned that the two dimensions interact. *That* they interact is a constant; *how* they interact is a cultural variable. Intimate bonds between family members, between friends, and between patrons and clients are the principal means of *organizing* communities under aristocracies, not to mention political machines. (This is why, when his son was about to make his debut in Roman public life, Marcus Tullius Cicero wrote him a handbook on the theory and practice of reciprocal personal obligation.)[17] Intimate bonds tend to *attenuate* attachments to the community under liberal regimes. (This is why Alexis de Tocqueville warned that democracy makes men draw into their private circles and let the public good take care of itself.)[18] Finally, intimate bonds are *systematically subverted* under totalitarianism. (And this is why, in the Soviet Union and People's Republic of China, citizens are invited to inform upon one another.)

Thus: Aristocrats—and machine "bosses"—tend to think of justice as doing good to friends and harm to enemies (one of the few points over which Pericles and Richard J. Daly might have seen eye to eye; though he rejected the idea, even Aristotle must have had it in mind when he said that if all of the members of a city were "friends," there would be no need for justice among them).[19] Likewise, liberals tend to think of justice as doing good to friends and being indifferent to everyone else, and finally, totalitarians tend to think of it as being indifferent to friends. The totalitarian balance is irremediably worse than the other two—but none of them is very attractive.

Flawed though they may be, the balances these communities

actually achieve can hardly fail to provide starting points (and dead weights) for reflection on the balances they ought to achieve. I cannot see where reflection on the comprehensive human good can possibly lead under a totalitarian regime, except to the necessity for its destruction. However, on the possibly fallacious assumption that neither aristocratic nor liberal regimes are equally hostile to the realization of the human good, we may at least distinguish all four of these from one another:

1 the interpretation of the excellences that is appropriate to an aristocratic community;
2 the interpretation of the excellences that an aristocratic community is likely to develop, left to itself;
3 the interpretation of the excellences that is appropriate to a liberal community; and
4 the interpretation of the excellences that a liberal community is likely to develop, left to itself.

"The essence of the lawgiver's art," said Tocqueville, "is by anticipation to appreciate these natural bents of human societies in order to know where the citizens' efforts need support and where there is more need to hold them back. For different times make different demands. The goal alone is fixed, to which humanity should press forward; the means of getting there ever change."[20]

A theory like Aristotle's can absorb criticisms of this kind provided that its structure is modified as shown in the Diagram 5.

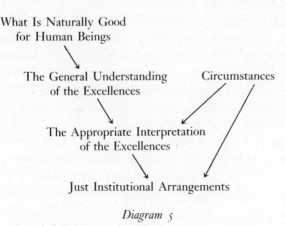

Diagram 5

As the preceding discussion may have suggested, modifying the scheme in this way vastly expands the notion of "circumstances." Neither in the contemporary forms of liberal theory nor in the original form of Aristotle's theory are circumstances taken to encompass anything so broad as what we now call "political culture." Among other things, this may even include unsound philosophical theory, prevailing misappropriations of sound philosophical theory, and all sorts of other historical residues. Aristotle could afford to be unhistorical. In no small part because of the profound changes wrought in Western political culture by the success of Aristotle and his contemporaries in inventing political philosophy, we cannot. But I hope it may go without further comment that the politics of virtues can be historical without being "historicist."

Now about all of this, the liberal is apt to say: "You have ameliorated my lesser doubts, but fed the greatest doubt of all. How reluctantly your great proponent of the politics of virtues yielded to the claims of the many and of the few! It was a part of virtue, he said, so to do, but at heart Aristotle was still an elitist, and that grave problem is yet to be addressed."

Excellence and Distribution

The case for labeling the politics of virtues as "elitist" is (a) its alleged premise that when circumstances permit, excellence of character should be the *only* distributive criterion, and (b) the argument that when excellence of character is the only distributive criterion, *any* degree of inequality and humiliation may be justified by those in power. I will present the case for the defense in the order opposite to the indictment. First, I will argue that even if excellence of character really were the only distributive criterion, no greater inequality could be justified than under liberal principles. Second I will raise questions about whether a purist attitude toward distributive criteria is really what the politics of virtues demands.

To begin: the first point that I should like to make is that using excellence of character as a distributive criterion does not just mean *rewarding* the excellences: it also means encouraging their development and eliciting their expression. In fact, encouraging their development and eliciting their expression are the principal reasons for rewarding them in the first place. To be sure, there is something to be said for rewarding the community's greatest benefactors "just because they deserve it"—and that *is* probably the greatest part of what Aristotle had in mind—but there is not as much to be said for it as one might suppose. The fact is that *no* human being *really* achieves the highest excellence or lives up to the highest standard his gifts and circumstances permit, neither those who receive rewards, those who dole them out, nor those who are lost in the shuffle. Therefore, making too much of intrinsic desert tempts us to a sanctimonious hypocrisy that is the very opposite of excellence.

I would offer the further argument that Aristotle was catastrophically wrong about the "great-souled man," the man with a high-minded sense of his own deserts:[21] the very best among us tend to be the least interested in external rewards. The ones whom the promise of reward may spur on to greater excellence are the ones whose excellence is in the greatest need of being spurred on. It is a kind of virtuous trick, which can easily develop into a pathology whereby we trick ourselves right out of what we are trying to trick ourselves into.

As to "eliciting the expression" of the excellences, rewards include offices, and offices certainly ought to go to those who know what they are doing and who are best able to organize the good qualities of others. But reward is not the only way to elicit the expression of the excellences any more than it is the only way to encourage their development; it is not even the only way of *using the distribution of goods* to further these two ends, as we shall see. At the point where rewards *cease* to further these two ends, they become excessive and must be capped.

Obviously, *any* effort to reward the excellences will authorize *some* inequality; but how much? Besides the rightly more advantaged and the rightly less advantaged, let us define the truly poor. The truly poor are those who are deprived of the material preconditions for the development of their natural gifts, or who receive such a raw deal in contrast with others that anyone with characteristically human emotional makeup would, in their shoes, suffer grievously from such corrosives as envy, sullenness, and despair.

True poverty cannot be defined in terms of sheer level of income. Level of opportunity comes closer, but even here, the particular opportunities to be deprived of which would make one truly poor are probably cultural variables. A rule of thumb that has a good ring to it (although it will scarcely satisfy those who hunger and thirst after mathematical precision) is that anyone who cannot participate meaningfully in the moral life of the total community is truly poor.

Now here is an axiom: an inequality which is so great as to withhold the material preconditions for the cultivation of excellence from anyone, or to discourage anyone from its cultivation by arousing irresistible envy, sullenness, or despair, is never any more effective in drawing forth good qualities from those whom it *does* advantage than a lesser inequality may be; in fact, it may even have the opposite effect of nourishing a callous or cynical attitude on the part of the well-off toward those in distress. And here is a definition: the *feasibility condition* for assistance is that means exist to help the truly poor that do more good to them than harm. Finally, here is a theorem: to the extent that the feasibility condition is met, true poverty cannot be justified under the politics of virtues. *One* of the ways in which the distribution of goods can be used to nourish the excellences is to guarantee the material preconditions for their development and to ameliorate just a few of the causes of envy, sullenness, and despair. We need not be egalitarian, but we must be merciful.

Whoever accepts the axiom must accept the theorem, but not everyone will accept the axiom. Nietzsche, for instance, regarded excellence of character as a "hothouse plant," a rare bloom of culture that can develop only when there are also "slaves."[22] What were his reasons? Did he read the data differently than some of us might? No, but he meant something different by "excellence." Under some circumstances he even thought callousness and cynicism to be commendable. The problem was that his understanding of excellence was distorted by an obsession with "mastery," and of course it is easy to think that in order to be "masterful," one must be a veritable master.

But what about Aristotle? Didn't he also believe that some men are "slaves by nature"?[23] Yes, he did. Now I do not believe that slaves by nature exist, nor that we could identify them if they did except by giving them a decent crack at life with everyone else. But suppose that we *could* identify them by other means. Even then, it would not make as much difference as one might think. For would we really want to argue that such men had no natural gifts at all? or that they were so insensible that they could feel neither envy, sullenness, nor despair? or that they were such unmen that to feel these passions would do their souls no damage? Surely we would not want to argue in this way, and so we would have to confront the axiom on its own territory. Could we really argue that it would be *necessary* for the nurture of the advantaged to burst the hearts of these poor souls or deprive them of the opportunities to nurture such small gifts as they did possess? I cannot see how we could, because I cannot see that it would. That is far from saying that I know how such beings *could* properly be dealt with, but we are not yet in Huxley's world of Alphas, Betas, Gammas, Deltas, and Epsilons, and, thank God, the problem does not yet face us.

Other axioms demand to be inscribed beneath the first. For instance, even a moderate inequality is detrimental to the cultivation of excellence when those who have the advantages have had to abuse others in order to get them (call that axiom two); and, superior advantages cannot encourage the cultivation of excellence unless those who receive them are also taught to regard themselves as under heavy obligation to the rest of society simply by virtue of receiving them (call that axiom three). Rewards should be thought of as a desirable burden; and this, incidentally, is the *only* way they could ever be made attractive to the *really* excellent among us.

But I will not discuss such axioms in detail; indeed, I can already hear the objection. "You call these axioms?" my interlocutor demands. "They aren't axioms; they're merely contingent assumptions." Yes, I suppose so, but there are contingencies and contingencies. It is difficult to see how some contingencies could fail to hold unless human nature itself were different, and although we can *imagine* that—what it would be like if we laid eggs and ate our young, for example—it is not the kind of mental experiment that is likely to be useful. I claim that my contingent assumptions are of this kind—and *that* is the kind of contingent assumption that no moral theory could do without, unless (as Rawls has said) it were to be founded wholly on definitions and tautologies.

Of course, if someone *did* want to reject my contingent assumptions, then certainly he *could* justify any degree of inequality and humiliation whatsoever—depending on his own contingent assumptions. But we can do the same thing within liberalism, if we are allowed to construe "property rights" in just the right way. Should we moderns ever get around to the attempt to reduce rhetoric to a science again,[24] surely these will be its first and second laws: *any set of basic principles can be made to yield any conclusion*, provided that we may choose secondary principles and interpretive rules just as we please; and *any set of secondary principles and interpretive rules can also be made to yield any conclusion*, provided that we have unlimited privileges to tinker with basic principles. Therefore, the aim in framing basic principles should not be to make them tamperproof, as modern analytical philosophers often seem to assume, but to make them true. And just as qualities of character should be nurtured in a form that anticipates the judgments individuals will one day have to make, so principles must be expressed in a form that anticipates the qualities of character of those by whom they will be applied. By the way, that is not merely a rhetorical aside but, as I see it, another premise of the politics of virtues. It follows from my previous analysis of the rational unity of motive.

Thus far, I have argued to the effect that even if excellence of character really were the only distributive criterion whatsoever, no greater inequality could be justified than under liberal principles. Now, concerning whether a purist attitude toward distributive criteria is really what the politics of virtues demands.

In the first place, experience and judgment tell us that aristocracies of merit tend to ossify and to become arbitrary, high-handed, and callous, eventually destroying the qualities they set out to enshrine. But what does that imply? That for the sake of excellence, we should ignore considerations of excellence? That would be strange; but the phrase "for the sake of" alerts us that even here we are covertly using excellence as a criterion. The difference is that we are no longer proposing its use as a *first-order* criterion. A first-order criterion is one by which goods are actually distributed. A second-order criterion is merely one that tells us what the first-order criteria are "for the sake of," so that we may tailor them to their ultimate objects. When we say that the politics of virtues gives first place to considerations of excellence, we need not mean that excellence of character is our only *first*-order criterion; in fact, nothing prevents us from *excluding* it from the list of first-order criteria. What we do mean is that excellence of character is at least at the top of our list of *second*-order criteria.[25]

For illustration, consider just one of the kinds of goods we may distribute; one that happens to be very important in liberal thought. I mean rights and liberties. Earlier I mentioned the view that the politics of virtues endangers the liberal ideals of liberty and equality. More precisely, Rawls states that the *equality of rights and liberties* can never be secure under a regime that gives first place to considerations of excellence of character. Now this would be true if excellence of character were a first-order criterion. But as I hope to show, it is false when excellence of character serves only as a second-order criterion. And it is absurd anyway, because, like the equality of property, the equality of rights and liberties is not now and never has been a liberal principle, although it has often been a liberal slogan. Surely no liberal imagines that you should have the same right to discipline my child that I have, or that I should have the same right to sell your house that you have, or that either of us should have the same liberty to speak before the U.S. House of Representatives as the individual whom we have elected to Congress.

What liberals have really taught and practiced, purged of the rhetoric, is something like this:

1 Criteria for the distribution of different kinds of rights and liberties to individuals should vary, and may include the following criteria among others:
   a *Relationship.* Rights and liberties distributed according to this criterion include (for instance) the exemption from being required to testify against a husband or wife, and the right to discipline one's own children within certain prescribed limits.

b   *Appointment*. Rights and liberties distributed according to this criterion include those belonging to legislators and to the chairs of joint stock corporations.

c   *Transaction*. Rights and liberties distributed according to this criterion include those acquired by contract, purchase, or gift.

d   *Membership*. Rights and liberties distributed according to this criterion include those acquired by citizenship or by belonging to a private association.

e   *Distress*. Rights and liberties distributed according to this criterion include those to which one acquires an "entitlement" by meeting the eligibility requirements for governmental public assistance programs.

f   *Capacity*. Rights and liberties distributed according to this criterion include all those that we deny in whole or in part to individuals who cannot exercise them without manifest harm to themselves or to others (for instance, children and the mentally handicapped).

g   *Retribution*. Rights and liberties distributed according to this criterion include all those that we deny in whole or in part to those who have violated the law. It is important to see how this criterion works: no matter how much we would like to rehabilitate criminals, make examples of them, or keep them out of situations where they may do wrong, we may not do *more* to them than they "deserve" for their offenses. We may do less, on account of either clemency or incompetence.

Are these first-order or second-order criteria? Clearly, they are first-order criteria, for with the possible exception of early natural rights theorists (and even here, the exception would be only partial), liberals have *also* provided us with criteria to *oversee* these criteria—that is, with *second*-order criteria that run something like this:

2   All distributions of rights and liberties should be subject to higher scrutiny, as follows:

a   To the greatest feasible degree, rights and liberties the exercise of which limits opportunities for other individuals to develop their capacities for rational self-direction should be so amended as to eliminate this tendency.

b Where elimination is not feasible, then to the greatest feasible degree, such exercises should be discouraged.

c "Feasibility" should be construed as consistency with the maintenance of a rough distinction between a "public" sphere, in which political action is presumed legitimate provided that the decision to take it has been made by constitutional means, and a "private" sphere, from which this presumption is absent.

Clearly this scheme is not hostile to all inequality in the distribution of rights and liberties—or even to most of it. What it discourages is the use of *ascriptive criteria* for unequal distribution; that is to say, the influence of characteristics like race, sex, and family is minimized.

But excellence is not an ascriptive criterion; no one is born with it. In fact, the interpretation of criterion 2(a) *demands* a doctrine of excellence of character, something that is vestigially present even in Locke's derivation of property rights in the fifth chapter of his *Second Treatise of Government*,[26] although it nearly vanishes from contemporary, "neutralist" versions of liberal theory.[27] To be sure, some liberals—first among them, John Stuart Mill—have proposed a more radical version of this first criterion:

a′ Rights and liberties should be generously distributed; only where they tend to interfere with one another should they be scaled back so as to eliminate this tendency.

And in this version, the criterion makes reference to nothing that can be construed in terms of excellence of character. No matter; we have merely passed from the second order to the *third* order, for in the *justification* of this criterion, Mill had very much indeed to say about human excellence and its development.[28]

Now proponents of the politics of virtues may differ as to the relative merits of the different versions of criterion 2(a), just as liberals may, but their disagreement will orbit around one issue: character. And an Aristotelian proponent of the politics of virtues would probably add to the set that includes the *first* version of criterion 2(a) another criterion like this:

d To the greatest degree consistent with *all* of the preceding criteria, rights and liberties should be so distributed as to offer scope for the exercise of virtue that is already manifest, and to encourage virtue that is not yet manifest.

This brings the regard for excellence back down from the third to the second order (although still not to the first). I suppose that liberals could accept criterion 2(d), but they would probably disagree with Aristotle over another issue in the politics of virtues, which we may call "management style."

Aristotle assumes—perhaps I should say "seems to assume," since I am forcing the text a little—that all institutions, in their distributive aspects as well as in all other aspects, need to be kept under a steady public gaze. Not only in the founding of a regime but at every moment thenceforth, the statesman is to ask, "What habits does this institution develop? What outlook does this criterion encourage? How is character educated overall?" For every institution is a school, and every experience bears a lesson, even if we wish it were not so; moreover, what forms us well in one generation may malform us in another, because long-range, compounded influences on character cannot be anticipated with perfect assurance and because external circumstances are always changing. By contrast, the assumption of a *liberal* politics of virtues is that the "invisible hand" is effective not only in the regulation of the economy but also—even more!—in the regulation of character, as Adam Smith tried to argue in his *Theory of Moral Sentiments*.[29] Subpolitical institutions such as the family, private property, and so forth will on this view best educate character when they are left alone, and are most safely left alone when the individuals involved in them have good character. Thus public action is necessary only (a) to maintain the background conditions that *enable* them to work by themselves, and (b) to intervene on those rare occasions when—because of unanticipated, exogenous influences—they are *obviously* not working as they should.

This liberal assumption is what lies behind criterion 2(c), which affirms the relative autonomy of subpolitical institutions. Of course, a liberalism that does *not* honor considerations of excellence may *also* affirm the relative autonomy of subpolitical institutions, but in this case the affirmation is freestanding. It is affirmed all right, but we don't know why. So, the background conditions that have to be assured before the relative autonomy of subpolitical institutions can even begin to make sense are poorly understood, and what it could mean for subpolitical institutions to malfunction—however rarely or frequently this may occur—is not fully thought through.

What we are beginning to see is that although not all versions of the politics of virtues are liberal, some versions of liberalism are consistent with the politics of virtues. Or are they? The imaginary interlocutor whom I left behind several pages ago must have been in a quiet simmer all this time. Given half a chance, he will surely burst out again: "You've been scoring points against a straw man. Why don't you put a real player in the game? True, liberals don't really teach or practice the necessary equality of every last right and liberty. But they *do* proclaim the necessary equality of *basic* rights and liberties. Using your idiom, these are the ones distributed according to the criterion of 'membership,' because in order to enjoy them one need only be a citizen of the political community. Can the politics of virtues give me the same assurance?"

Very well, let's examine the case for guaranteeing an equality in *one* place that we do not guarantee in *every* place.

Excellence and Citizenship

Sometimes, those who favor an equality of basic rights and liberties paraphrase their conviction by saying that members of the community should not be divided into "first-class citizens" and "second-class citizens." This is a little bit misleading—and suggests a confusion in the very idea of an equality of basic rights and liberties. Under the American liberal regime, for example, not everyone may vote: only those who have attained a certain age, who can establish residency in a certain district, and who register. Obviously, we do divide citizens into classes. But again, we minimize the use of *ascriptive criteria* for this classification. Taking up residence in a voting district and going down to register are voluntary acts. No one can do anything about his age, but at least youth is not a permanent civic disability—if you wait long enough, it goes away. So although not everyone is in the first class of citizens, *anyone may get into it*; put another way, although not everyone is admitted to first-class rights, *everyone has the right to acquire them*. What this shows is that we must answer two questions, not one, and neither is the same as the question with which we began. The question with which we began—whether we ought to classify citizens—is trivial, because every conceivable regime would do so. What we really need to know is, first, whether the classification of the citizens ought to be based on ascription or achievement and, second, what the ascriptive criteria *or* standards of achievement should be.

That there is a *single* liberal answer to *either* of these questions is a myth. Contemporary liberals hold, by and large, that the classification of citizens ought to be based on achievement, not ascription, and that the standards of achievement ought to be trivially easy to satisfy (like the voting requirements noted above). But historically speaking, the liberal aversion to ascriptivity has been less in the nature of an outright ban than a way of placing the burden of proof; thus John Locke was perfectly willing to accept the ascriptive institutions of the Crown and hereditary nobility, *provided* that they enjoyed the consent of the population as a whole.[30] In the second place, the aversion to high standards of achievement has not been common to all liberals; thus the earliest liberals protected their republics by restricting the suffrage to those who owned property, on the grounds that a man who was dependent upon another for his living was in no position to maintain his independence in politics (alternatively, that if he *could* maintain his independence, his vote would voice his envy). In the third place, liberal principles have sometimes been held to apply only under ideal circumstances; thus John Stuart Mill, a proponent of the politics of virtues as well as a liberal, claimed that a population afflicted by an "inveterate spirit of locality" was unfit to govern itself, and could learn the concept of the "common good" only under the reign of a centralizing monarch.[31]

Now I do not know whether the answer of *contemporary* liberals to the two questions at hand is true or false, so I do not think I should be compelled to show that proponents of the politics of virtues *must* give the same answer as they do. But proponents of the politics of virtues *may* give answers just as various as those that liberals in general have given—depending upon their reading of the political facts—and it may be of some use to show how they might reason.

To begin with, could the politics of virtues justify a purely ascriptive classification of citizens, as under a hereditary aristocracy? Yes, but not as easily as it was justified by the liberal Locke. He required only consent; into the reasons for which a sovereign people might reasonably give or withhold consent, he did not far inquire. But a proponent of the politics of virtues would have to know the reasons. He would have to be shown grounds for believing that a hereditary aristocracy advances the virtues of the citizenry as a whole.

One argument might run something like this. Wherever there is a political community, subordination is inevitable: some must rule, while others follow. Thus the question arises, who should be admitted to rulership? If rulers are *not* selected according to birth, then they must be selected in some other way. Now birth may be arbitrary, but it may be argued that the nobly born are at least as likely to be competent as they are to be incompetent, especially since they are trained for the exercise of authority from childhood. By contrast, every other method of selection is less likely to produce competent than incompetent rulers. Examination, for instance, might be a good way to fill the lesser ranks of the civil bureaucracy, but it is certainly not a good way to choose lawgivers, because it emphasizes good memory over genuine practical wisdom. Popular election is even worse, because only a pander can win the multitude; over the sentiments of the crowd, good memory holds no greater force of attraction than wisdom, for neither can compete with a lying promise. Another merit of rule by birth is that precisely because it *is* arbitrary—as arbitrary as the location of the sea or the time of the rainfall—no one can feel slighted; one comes to accept it in the same way that one accepts other accidents of nature. Thus the nobility should have no more grounds for pride than have the commoners for envy.

Of course, each and every one of these claims may also be challenged from the selfsame perspective of virtue. (1) Against the claim that the nobly born are at least as likely to be competent as incompetent, we may reply that *in*competence is far more likely, because among the nobly born it cannot lead to loss of rank. (2) Against the affirmation of the advantages of being raised to rule, we may reply that we cannot speak of education in virtue in the same way that we speak of education in, say, arithmetic. Practical wisdom can be cultivated and encouraged, but not taught.[32] (3) Against the claim that one comes to accept arbitrary distinctions of rank in the same way that one accepts accidents of nature, we may reply that this is precisely how people become convinced of their "natural" superiority or inferiority. Although this involves a play on the term "Nature," logic is not ordinarily strong enough to halt either vanity or self-contempt. The result? The nobly born will fancy themselves gods; the commoners will become either brutishly passive or inflamed with envy—the first when they submit to the pretenses of the nobility, the second when they do not.

A fourth argument carries us from defense to offense. From earliest times, following the lead of Aristotle, proponents of the politics of virtues have held that man is by nature a political animal: that is, a being who can only attain his full measure by taking part in thought and debate over the common good.[33] If this is true, then to restrict the practice of deliberation to the nobly born would compromise the humanity of the commoners. It would deny them the material conditions for developing excellence of character; it would make them truly poor. And this the politics of virtues cannot abide.

Could advocates of a hereditary aristocracy make reply to these objections? Yes, I think so, but it would require difficult and perhaps dubious empirical claims to counter those of their critics. They would be more prudent to amend their proposal. A "mixed" regime, in which nobles and commoners divide the exercise of sovereignty between them, might capture the advantages of a "pure" hereditary aristocracy while escaping its defects. Just so, Locke pictured the British constitution in his *Second Treatise*. But just to the degree that this amended proposal persuades, it raises the possibility that a further amendment might make it even more persuasive. Although the Senate, as established by the Constitution of the United States, is not an ascriptive institution, clearly the founders of that mixed regime intended it to resemble one. To enter the Senate is more difficult than to enter the House of Representatives, and its term of office is three times as long. While most of the considerations the *Federalist* advances in its favor would equally serve the cause of a hereditary upper chamber, those that are left over tend to show the relative advantage of an elected upper house.[34]

Here, of course, we are already talking about something more than the simple twofold classification of citizens described before. To begin with, we have fourth-class citizens who are not eligible to vote at all. Third-class citizens are eligible to vote but not to hold office. Second-class citizens are eligible to hold office as well as to vote. First-class citizens actually hold office. Getting out of the fourth class into the third depends partly on ascriptive criteria (age) and partly on achievements (registration). Getting out of the third class into the second depends on further ascriptive criteria (age, and also nativity: the President may not be a naturalized citizen although holders of other offices may). Getting out of the second class into the first depends on an increasingly difficult achievement (obtaining appointment or election).

This betrays a striking movement in our reflections. Not more than a few paragraphs ago we junked the question whether we ought to classify citizens at all, in favor of the questions whether the classification of the citizens ought to be based on ascription or achievement, and what the ascriptive criteria or standards of achievement should be. Now, this issue of how to classify citizens seems to be collapsing into the issue of how to choose between regimes. Over and above what was said at the beginning of the chapter, is there any way to get a handle on this issue?

Excellence and the Fundamental Question

To "get a handle" on the issue of choice between regimes is possible, but I cannot go further here. At that, getting a handle on the *issue* is not the same as knowing, in Lenin's words, "what is to be done." For instance, should liberal regimes turn out to be less than ideal even under our own cultural circumstances, it would not necessarily follow that we should make a revolution! Still, even if ideality is not among our options, trying to approach it in theory may help us to understand the options we do have. So let us proceed. If we had a genie to gather for us all the data we presently lack, how would we use this data in order to choose between regimes?

Let us begin by defining a few terms. First, let's distinguish between classes of citizens that are "formally deliberative" and classes of citizens that are not. A class of citizens is formally deliberative if effective deliberation concerning the common good is included among the constitutional responsibilities of its members. By "effective" I mean that the class is not merely advisory; rather, the constitution provides that by their acts the members of this class may direct, or at least constrain, some of the business of the regime. I should also mention that the assignment of a responsibility to the members of a class does not establish a presumption that they actually fulfill this responsibility. Applying these criteria, we find that under the American regime, the first, second, and third classes are formally deliberative, but the fourth class is not.

Next, let us distinguish between ascriptive characteristics that are "superable" and ascriptive characteristics that are "insuperable." An ascriptive characteristic is insuperable if it is permanent and unalterable; otherwise, it is superable. Race is an insuperable ascriptive characteristic. Youth, by contrast, is superable. Selection by lots for life is insuperable, but selection by lots for fixed terms—a practice of the ancient Greek democracies—is superable. Family is ordinarily insuperable, but where commoners can be adopted into noble families, we would surely call it superable. Adult adoption into the great houses of Rome was a fairly common practice.

Finally, we need to decide what we mean by a "republic." Let us say that in order to be called by that name, a regime must at least forgo the use of insuperable ascriptive criteria for dividing the formally deliberative classes from the others. We will also call republics "generous" when they implement one or both of the following measures. The first is to make the *remaining* criteria for dividing the formally deliberative classes from the others trivially easy to satisfy. Establishing residency is a trivial achievement compared with acquiring a certain amount of property; and although of the two ascriptive criteria, youth and family, neither is insuperable (at least not when adult adoption is permitted), still the former is trivial compared with the latter. The *second* measure is to forgo the use of insuperable ascriptive criteria, *not only* in dividing the formally deliberative classes from the others *but also* in dividing the higher of the constitutionally deliberative classes from the lower. The American republic is generous in the first sense but not in the second, because no one may be elected to the office of President who is not a natural-born citizen, and this ascriptive criterion is insuperable.

Notice that this is a very thin way of using the term "republic"—not to mention the term "generous." It admits to republichood all sorts of regimes that contemporary liberals do not like to call republics—such as the Roman "republic" and one-party "republics"—and some of these regimes are pretty foul. But considering our momentary focus on citizenship, this way of speaking will suffice. What we need now is to figure out how to ask (a) whether the liberal expectation is plausible that all other things being equal, republics make better regimes than others, and (b) whether the *contemporary* liberal expectation is plausible that all other things being equal, *generous* republics are better still. What I mean by "figure out how to ask" is that I am not going to answer these two questions. Rather I am interested in how to frame them in such ways that, with further empirical investigation, proponents of the politics of virtues *could* answer them. Political philosophers like to challenge the distinction between facts and values. But if they are serious about this, they had better begin speaking with political scientists who are willing to do the same.

Now so far as I am aware, there are only two ways in which proponents of the politics of virtues have gone about asking what counts as a good regime. The first way is Aristotle's, the second is Mill's. These two ways are similar, but not identical. Aristotle begins by noting that the "good citizen" is someone who is understood to contribute to the life of his community. Under an oligarchy the best citizen is the rich man; under a martial regime, the soldier—and so on. By contrast, the "good man" is in principle the same everywhere, at least in broad outline.[35] If poor upbringing or bad will has not depraved us, we recognize him at once: this is the man whose life is marked by rational purpose and self-understanding; who has depth, commitment, and a kind of transparency to himself and others. Now if being a good man and being a good citizen were completely *independent* of one another, we could forget about being good citizens and bend all that is within us to being good men. (This despite Machiavelli, who proposed that we forget about being good men and bend all that is within us to being good citizens.)

But things are not that simple. "Independence" is a two-way street. We know that we can be good citizens in a purely relativistic sense without being good men and women, but can we be good men and women without being good citizens? The answer is that we can, but that something important will be lacking. The *kind* of depth, commitment, and transparency that is proper to human beings requires that we *share* in rational purposes with others, and seek *with* them an understanding of the common good. We need the political community, and if the real one doesn't permit us to do these things, we have to make one up in our heads—as Plato did. The kind of regime that *does* permit us to do these things can be succinctly described as the one in which the good human being is the uniquely best citizen as well, and that is nothing more nor less than Aristotle's criterion. We can hardly ever satisfy it—he admits that—but we can use it as a benchmark or, to shift the metaphor, as an instrument: an instrument with which to probe the possibilities and limits of the regimes in which we find ourselves, and to compare them with such alternatives as may from time to time be within reach of common action.

Mill's criterion we have seen already. He begins with the observation that every regime has two sides, one "educational," the other "mechanical." The best regime under given circumstances is the one that is most nearly perfect from both sides—that does the best job circumstances permit of developing good qualities in the citizens, and also does the best job circumstances permit of organizing the good qualities already existing in order to carry out the public business. This criterion has both advantages and disadvantages in comparison with Aristotle's:

1 A *disadvantage* is that it tempts us to think of "good qualities" as though they could coexist in any permutation or combination, either with one another or with qualities that are not so good; it imparts no sense of the functional dependence of imperfectly developed excellences and complementary defects—of the way in which they hang together in a whole personality.

2 A compensating *advantage* is that the criterion shakes us out of an impression Aristotle all too easily gives, that there is but a single way in which the excellences *can* hang together, a single all-round good personality—as though all good people were identical, eyelash to toenail; as though they did not grow more and more fully unique as they grew more and more virtuous. But perhaps we could have had this advantage of Mill's criterion without the disadvantage it accompanies.

3 There is also an *uncompensated* disadvantage, that Mill alludes to two contrasting understandings of human flourishing in this selfsame criterion. The mention of good qualities involves his theory of rational thriving, which has roots in Aristotle. By contrast, utilitarian doctrine was that to thrive is to feel pleasure, and that the public business is to foment that pleasure and spread it around—an idea in which Mill also concurred, or thought he did.[36]

4 Finally, there is an uncompensated *advantage*: that Mill's criterion tears us loose from the world of definition, plunging us into the world of arms and legs and warm minds and passions. Whereas Aristotle asks who *is* the best citizen in

any given regime, Mill asks two much more cogent questions: which qualities the regime *engenders*, and which qualities it *knows how to use*.

Since certain advantages are peculiar to each of these criteria, there would be little point in choosing one over the other. Instead, suppose we reform Mill's criterion under an Aristotelian inspiration. The result is a compound criterion something like this:

> What are the different kinds of characters that a particular kind of regime tends to produce? (And how near are they to any of the recognizable species of "good men"?)

> What are the different kinds of characters that the particular kind of regime tends to *use* in ways that befit and exercise their virtues? (And does it use all those it produces?)

The parenthetical questions are the ones that help us discover what good there may be in a regime; the questions them precede them set them up. Unfortunately, what this new criterion gains in comprehensiveness, it loses in ease of handling. Aristotle's criterion was simple and elegant. It asked only one question: How far is the "good citizen" of regime X, Y, or Z from being a "good man"? By answering this question over and over until he ran out of regimes, eventually Aristotle should have been able to place every regime whatsoever (not counting regimes not yet invented) in a single order of rank. Although this ordering would be "weak," in that some regimes might occupy the same ranks, it would at least be "complete," in that every regime would be comparable to every other. By contrast, Mill asked *two* questions. Ordinarily, we would expect the answers to generate two distinct orderings, a problem Mill got around by tacitly assuming that both of them converged on a single apex (at which he claimed to find "representative government"). The new criterion *also* asks two questions; what is worse, each of them requires comparing *sets* of character types rather than simple pairs, as under Aristotle's criterion. Whatever the means one might use in order to mash all the necessary acts of judgment into a single order of rank, odds are that this ordering will be either extremely weak (that is to say, sharing ranks will be the rule rather than the exception), or incomplete (that is to say, some regimes will be simply incomparable to some other regimes). It may even be both extremely weak *and* incomplete. Mill's strategy for reducing the dimensions of the analytical problem—focusing on the apex—could still be followed, but any incomplete ordering may have more than one apex, between which no comparisons whatsoever may be made.

Suppose we have done all of this anyway; more precisely, suppose we have done it again and again and again, once for every set of cultural circumstances that concerns us—a truly Herculean labor. *Only then* are we in a position to ask our fundamental questions about citizenship and the choice of regime, which can finally be put in just nine words:

Is a republic at each apex?

Is it generous?

If "yes" both times, then contemporary liberals are partly vindicated. If "yes" the first time but "no" the second, then some liberals may make their peace with the politics of virtues, but they will not include the liberals of the contemporary school. If "no" from the start, then perhaps liberalism is wrong.

CHAPTER FIVE

Nature Compromised

The politics of virtues, as discussed in Chapter 4, may well seem preposterous to anyone familiar with human vices. Chapter 5 takes this objection seriously but shows that modern strategies for escaping the demands of the politics of virtues are not only preposterous but dangerous. Like Scylla and Charybdis, these twin problems hem the ship of theory on left and right. The chapter concludes by considering the outmost limits to its forward advance.

The Trouble with Virtue

The trouble with virtue is that it is practically nowhere to be found. Since Machiavelli, one of our favorite slogans has been that we should "take man as he really is" rather than as we might imagine that he ought to be.[1] The early moderns rebelled against religious doctrines of virtue which (they thought) made unnatural demands in order to feed a horrified disgust for passionate human nature. The religious adversary is now considered dead, but the rebellion has become institutionalized. For the following diatribe we are indebted to the spleen of Lord Macaulay:

> The boast of the ancient philosophers was that their philosophy formed the minds of men to a high degree of wisdom and virtue. . . . But the truth is that, in those very matters in which alone

they professed to do any good to mankind, in those very matters for the sake of which they neglected all the vulgar interests of mankind, they did nothing, or worse than nothing. They promised what was impracticable; they despised what was practicable; they filled the world with long words and long beards; and they left it as wicked and as ignorant as they found it.

An acre in Middlesex is better than a principality in Utopia. The smallest actual good is better than the most magnificent promises of impossibilities. The wise man of the Stoics would, no doubt, be a grander object than a steam-engine. But there are steam-engines. And the wise man of the Stoics is yet to be born.[2]

"From the testimony of friends as well as foes," he fulminates, "it is plain that these teachers of virtue had all the vices of their neighbors with the additional vice of hypocrisy."

Now to say that we should *not* take man as he really is would be daft. But *really* taking him as he is means taking him as a being in need of the excellences. To make no effort to cultivate them— to let the souls of the citizens grow wild and take them as we find them—is worse than daft. Lord Macaulay denied that he wanted "a world of water-wheels, power-looms, steam-carriages, sensualists, and knaves."[3] But he made it clear enough that he was willing to take the sensualists and knaves in return for the assurance of water-wheels, power-looms, and steam-carriages. In the meantime, the knaves have invented the balance of terror, the use of psychoactive drugs against political prisoners, and several varieties of Holocaust, while we sensualists have always been one step behind. One may be forgiven for wondering whether the bargain is getting worse instead of better.

Yet—just what *would* it take to shape the budding dispositions of the young in just such a way that they ripen perfectly into excellence? Merely to describe the regimen is enough to show it up as a dream. Presumably, the *first* step would be to form habits in the young by contriving situations that would elicit only the impulses we wish to reward, and in which these impulses would, in fact, be rewarded. That is easier said than done. As I have just put it, it sounds like simple operant conditioning. But even leaving questions of free will aside, human beings are not rats. What a child recognizes in a situation, what it anticipates, what it finds rewarding, all depend upon its previous experiences and its powers of imagination.

Consequently, the *second* step in the formation of virtue would have to be more invasive. We would contrive to provide suitable materials for imagination, eventually including appropriate ideals and examples. But what an immature mind makes of an example that is supposed to be inspiring may be drastically different from what an adult would make of it. Worse yet, the vehicle through which materials are presented powerfully shapes their engagement with imagination. The flashy McLuhanites were hardly the first to notice this. So Socrates stressed arational over rational elements in his discussion of music—rhythmic mode over content. And it may go without saying that the rational is easier to monitor than the arational.

And what about that rational content? This is the matter of the *third* step, which prefigures permanent and complete adult activity. We would contrive to intervene in the individual's unfolding reflections about himself and the world, giving them form, even to the point—where the opportunity presented itself—of offering arguments of principle. One of the things this obviously requires is the action of a moral teacher who can excite the imagination in the prospect and practice of virtue. But as the record shows, Socrates was no more likely to produce a Plato than an Alcibiades; nor Jesus of Nazareth, a Simon Peter than a Judas Iscariot.

There is more. Obviously each step in the cultivation of excellence involves a critique of the foundation set in the preceding step; some of the foundation must be broken up and recast in order for it to support a more ambitious structure. Complicating this is the fact that youthful dispositions develop at different rates in different dimensions. Even children have wants, have motives, tell stories about themselves; that is enough to begin cultivating *integral* excellence. But the cultivation of *intimate* excellence, upon which integral excellence is partly dependent, is always held back. This is because pity, romance, the desire to belong—in fact all the impulses that transport the young most irresistibly outside themselves—are not fully available until adolescence, and to force them upon the awareness too early is destructive (although once these impulses have made a beachhead, one is obliged to act quickly, or the opportunity to teach the child anything may be ruined). The cultivation of *political* excellence is more retarded still. Although many young people already feel the pull of the greater horizon, their incandescent imaginations must achieve a steadier glow and change in focus before they can balance the claims of the intimate against the claims of the political.

In Plato's mythical community, the problem of balance was "solved" by drastic means: the political was fused with the intimate by so altering human relationships that all citizens regarded themselves as relatives, and the intimate was fused with the integral by so diffusing the attachments of the citizens to their own bodies that each felt the pains and pleasures of every other as his own. On top of that, the natural and the conventional were made to disappear into each other without residue by convincing the citizens of their physical kinship with their native soil.[4] Dream on! In the real world, such balance as we achieve is wrung from moral crises. Few of us clearly remember how, as children, we wondered why we should control ourselves at all— but we did so wonder. Most of us remember the crisis of adolescence rather well: why should I care about anyone else—and just how is that done? The third crisis scarcely needs calling to mind, since it often remains a preoccupation of adulthood: why should I be just—and how is it even possible? As to the fourth crisis, the absolute antagonism between Nature and culture is a canon of what we moderns like to call philosophy. No wonder moral education cannot guarantee its results; and no wonder the ancient philosophers, by bringing these questions to awareness, ran the risk of making well enough worse.

So real excellence is apt to be a rare item, more like leaven than like flour. Cultivating the excellences will always be of the first importance, but we should also be prepared to curb and channel the flows and eruptions of passion. This is where all the brilliance of the sixteenth through eighteenth centuries was lavished. We *are* passionate beings, and though the men of that age erred in thinking that *only* the passions needed their attention, we can still learn from them. Indeed, we had better, because our inherited institutions nourish their errors as well as their insights. If classical political theory was aimed at the health of the soul, then modern political theory has been based on neurotic stabilization; and as every good political therapist knows, we need each in order to know the limits of the other.

The Promises of Passion

To one degree or another, every individual is deficient in the excellences. Recalling that the excellences are dispositions whereby every passion (and capacity) is called upon "at the right time, toward the right objects, toward the right people, for the right reason, and in the right manner," the most dramatic consequence of this deficiency is that often various passions are active when they should be dormant, and dormant when they should be active. How can political order be maintained without virtue? Here enters the most important *tacit* assumption of modern thought: that without virtue, activating a dormant passion is a lot less trouble than quieting an active one. This leads to a fateful but equally tacit decision: that social control should depend as much as possible upon activating dormant passions, and as little as possible on quieting active ones. Although the terminology of "virtue" is for a while retained, the cultivation of excellence gradually ceases to be a goal. The new goal is to associate passions with objects and occasions in such a way as to limit the damage done by passions whose activity is taken for granted, while in the meantime satisfying our characteristic desires as well as may be.

There are at least four means by which this may be done. The first three were also known to the classical writers, although I will concentrate on their modern versions. The last was not discussed at all until the modern era. In the following sections I sketch them each in turn before changing direction for the conclusion.

Substitution

The first strategy is to find dispositions that are easier to cultivate than the excellences but that produce the same outward behavior when circumstances are just right. Plato, for instance, noticed that the anger of men with a keen sense of honor can simulate the virtue of justice.[5] This way of using the "spirited" impulses recalls my remarks in the Mezzalogue on the proto-virtues; thus it should come as no surprise that what the first strategy often comes down to is giving the proto-virtues the name of virtue proper and declaring them good enough. Hence the name "substitution."

Adam Smith offered a systematic development of this strategy in his *Theory of Moral Sentiments*, which is one of the least-read classics of the modern era.[6] At the core of the book is "Sympathy." Smith meant much more by this term than, for instance, our tendency to feel sorry for those in distress; in fact, he argued that those in distress sympathize with their witnesses no less than their witnesses sympathize with them. He believed that the perception of a concordance between one's own sentiments and the sentiments of another always produces pleasure, even when the sentiments themselves are unpleasant.[7] By contrast, the perception of a discordance between one's own sentiments and the sentiments of another always produces pain, even when the sentiments themselves are pleasant. However, psychological pain is an *innately* unstable condition. Therefore, without any initial need for conscious direction, the mind always acts to modify its state so that the difference between its own sentiments and those of the persons present to it is lessened. Sympathy is precisely this movement of the passions in the direction of concordance.[8]

Any two people placed in each other's presence will tend to sympathize with each other in this special sense. However, this does not necessarily mean that their passions will be so modified as to meet in the middle. Some feelings are innately more difficult to sympathize with than others.[9] This has two consequences. The first is that usually one will modify his feelings more than the other, with the result that any concordance of sentiment the parties achieve is apt to be off center. The second is that concordance may not be reached at all. However, each of the parties is aware of the movement of passion in the other as well as in himself. If experience has taught one of the parties that his feelings are more difficult to sympathize with than those of the other, he is likely to modify his own feelings to a greater degree than he would otherwise in order to facilitate the other's sympathy. Obviously, then, the innate pleasure in the concordance of sentiments and the innate instability of painful states of mind pattern not only the way we feel but also the way we *learn* to feel. Since each of us continually plays both the role of spectator and the role of spectacle, given sufficient experience we learn two kinds of qualities:

> Upon these two different efforts, upon that of the spectator to enter into the sentiments of the person principally concerned, and upon that of the person principally concerned, to bring down his emotions to what the spectator can go along with, are founded two different sets of virtues. The soft, the gentle, the amiable virtues, the virtues of candid condescension and indulgent humanity, are founded upon the one: the great, the awful, and respectable, the virtues of self-denial, of self-government, of that command of the passions which subjects all the movements of our own nature to what our own dignity and honor, and the propriety of our own conduct, require, take their origin from the other.[10]

Now in the classical sense, the term "virtue" always designates a quality that contributes to our full and appropriate development, that completes or perfects our Nature, that sustains human flourishing. Smith's use of the term raises the question whether his understanding of the qualities he calls "virtues" is at all classical. Superficially, the answer is "yes"; at a deeper level, the answer is "no." He *does* have a notion of full and appropriate development: "And hence it is, that to feel much for others, and little for ourselves, that to restrain our selfish, and to indulge our benevolent, affections, constitutes the perfection of human nature; and can alone produce among mankind that harmony of sentiments and passions in which consists their whole grace and propriety."[11] But the implicit logic of this passage is that feeling much for others and little for ourselves is the "perfection" of human nature *only because* it contributes to a concordance of sentiments—and as we have already seen, the grace and propriety of this concordance lies *wholly* in the pleasure that it produces. For Smith, the criterion of human flourishing is a *pleasurable* activity of the soul rather than a *rational* activity of the soul: his doctrine of virtue rests on a hedonic foundation. True enough, he promotes a foreshortened kind of rational purposefulness and self-understanding—but as means to the end of pleasure, not for their intrinsic worth.

The second point in which Smith decisively departs from classical doctrine is in making the well-controlled rather than the well-disposed man his ideal. Truly Stoic language is called upon in praise of the virtues in his second set:

> The little sympathy we feel with bodily pain is the foundation of the propriety of constancy and patience in enduring it. The man who under the severest tortures, allows no weakness to escape him, vents no groan, gives way to no passion which we do not entirely enter into, commands our highest admiration. His firmness enables him to keep time with our indifference and insensibility. We admire and entirely go along with the magnanimous effort which he makes for this purpose.[12]

If we recall the tacit modern assumption that it is harder to quiet an active passion than to activate a dormant passion, Smith's emphasis becomes easier to understand. As it turns out, his words about the sufferer "bringing down" his emotions to a pitch with which the spectator can go along are misleading: what he really means is that the sufferer *represses* that portion of his emotions to which the spectator is indifferent. The repressed emotions do not go away. They cannot go away. They go underground.

Arguably, Smith's entire discussion so far has confused morals with manners. In detailing this repression, he continues to blur them. Initially, repression requires the physical presence of spectators. Eventually we become anxious not only to *have* approval—which spectators award us when they perceive the concordance between our sentiments and theirs—but also to *deserve* approval.[13] This sounds all right, but it does not mean what it seems to mean. All of the spectators whom the individual encounters are partial in one way or another; what one can approve, then, often differs from what another can approve. But with enough experience of partial spectators, the individual is able to generalize beyond the moment, to develop an enlarged view of matters, even to entertain the fancy of an Impartial Spectator who represents, as it were, the whole of humanity rather than the particular persons who may at any moment surround him.[14] By some peculiarity of imagination, this Impartial Spectator becomes an interior psychological agency with a personality of his own: "I divide myself," Smith explains, "into two persons."[15] The individual desires a concordance of sentiments with this interior person just as literally as he desires a concordance of sentiments with exterior persons. For Smith, then, becoming anxious not only to have approval but also to deserve approval means becoming anxious not only to have the approval of the men who surround me but also to have the approval of the "Man within the Breast."[16]

Smith's theory of the differentiation between the ordinary self and the second self resembles Freud's theory of the differentiation between the ego and the superego,[17] in that both are theories of introjection and identification. However, Freud parts sharply from Smith in assuming that a person identifies with *specific* exterior individuals rather than with a least common denominator for the whole of humanity. In his view these identifications are ways of giving up the hopeless libidinal attachments that preoccupy everyone during the Oedipal stage. What for Freud is a process of sublimation is for Smith a process of sympathy. (I will have more to say about sublimation later, but not in this context.)

Suppose for the sake of argument that Smith's theory accurately describes the workings of sympathy and the development of conscience. In wealth of detail and delicacy of articulation, it is certainly a match for any other, yet the wisdom of depending upon these processes remains in question. What guarantees that our sympathy will always be right? Won't our feelings be misled by those who surround us? Smith admits that this can happen but regards it as the exception rather than the rule. For a simple reason, he thinks, most people can be counted upon to do the right thing. The Impartial Spectator is really just an amalgam of all the partial spectators by whom one has been witnessed in the past. Therefore, in order to unhook ourselves from the moment and see ourselves as the entire world would see us, all we need is a fund of diverse life experiences. We are led, as though by an invisible hand, to feel as we ought to feel; no special effort of cultivation is required.

But if our experiences lack this breadth and diversity, won't the Man Within simply confirm us in our bondage to the man without—won't Impartiality be merely a more authoritative name for partiality? The answer is "yes," and as Hannah Arendt has told, this fate can even overtake an entire nation of ordinary people:

> And just as the law in civilized countries assumes that the voice of conscience tells everybody "Thou shalt not kill," even though man's natural desires and inclinations may at times be murderous, so the law of Hitler's land demanded that the voice of conscience tell everybody: "Thou shalt kill," although the organizers of the massacres knew full well that murder is against the normal desires and inclinations of most people. Evil in the Third Reich had lost the quality by which most people recognize it—the quality of temptation. Many Germans and many Nazis, probably an overwhelming majority of them, must have been tempted *not* to murder, *not* to rob, *not* to let their neighbors go off to their doom (for that the Jews were transported to their doom they knew, of course, even though many of them may not have known the gruesome details), and not to become accomplices in all these crimes by benefitting from them. But, God knows, they had learned to resist temptation.[18]

What holds for "conscience" holds for substitutional strategies in general. There is no reason to expect any other to be more reliable. As way stations, or as backups, the proto-virtues are indispensable. Confused with virtue proper, they carry a burden of peril.

Countervailance

The second strategy is to achieve a useful result by pitting some of the passions against others, not through the agencies of proto-virtues but directly. Thanks to Albert O. Hirschman's *The Passions and the Interests*,[19] this strategy has recently become well known under the name of "the principle of the countervailing passion."[20] I can scarcely hope to add anything to Hirschman's brilliant discussion of how, in the seventeenth century, the prospects for this strategy came to be systematically studied by thinkers who asked, "Is it not possible to discriminate among the passions and fight fire with fire—to utilize one set of comparatively innocuous passions to countervail another more dangerous and destructive set or, perhaps, to weaken and tame the passions by such internecine fights in *divide et impera* fashion?"[21] But I may hope to contribute a few hit-and-run theoretical remarks.

There is a striking resemblance, for instance, between passionate conflict and what animal ethologists call "stimulus conflict." Stimulus conflict occurs when stimuli that are associated with mutually incompatible responses are presented to an animal simultaneously. This is far from rare. Judging from the comments of Robert A. Hinde, a specialist in such matters, stimulus conflict is as ubiquitous among animals as passionate conflict is among humans.[22] Ethologists theorize that in the animal's nervous system, every response stands in an order of rank with respect to the others. This ranking is called "prepotency." What determines the order of prepotency in each situation is not well understood. However, the notion suggests that in situations of stimulus conflict, responses of the *same* prepotency block one another, so that the highest-ranked response among those remaining is the response that is expressed. To put this another way, there are three possibilities:

1   One response is highest in order of prepotency, so that it "trumps" all of the others.
2   All responses are equal in order of prepotency, so that the animal is simply immobilized: like a rabbit caught in the glare of approaching headlights, it freezes.
3   The most highly ranked responses deadlock, clearing the way for the expression of another response that is lower in order of prepotency. Thus the animal engages in behavior seemingly inappropriate to the situation, such as grooming.

Now there is a great difference between the passions of human beings and the emotional and behavioral responses of animals. In particular, the arousal of a man's passions, their relative intensity, and the form they take are likely to depend far less on what he sees than on (1) what he thinks he sees, (2) what he thinks *of* what he sees, and (3) what he thinks in general. Therefore, it would be foolish to put too fine a point on any analogy. However, the first possible outcome of stimulus conflict is *formally* similar to countervailance proper, while the second is *formally* similar to the strategy Hirschman calls *divide et impera*—"divide and rule." One can hardly resist asking whether the third possible outcome to stimulus conflict also has a counterpart in passionate conflict. The answer, I think, is that it does—and that the thinkers of the seventeenth century were willing to exploit the fact. In Hirschman's interpretation, it was the view of Hobbes that the way to the Social Contract is paved by the triumph of the calm passions involved in the calculation of material advantage over the unruly passions involved in the war of all against all. But Hobbes really seems to have seen matters the other way around. He regarded a deadlock between the opposing passions of fear and glory as a prerequisite for the expression of the passions involved in the pursuit of material advantage, for these passions are not only calm, but weak. In other words, whereas Hirschman sees Hobbes as exploiting the first possible outcome to passionate conflict, I see him as exploiting the third.

On the other hand, Hirschman is certainly right that the stress of most seventeenth-century thinkers was on the first device. He is also right to point out that this device was recognized in the early fifth century by Augustine—though in the first place what he calls Augustine's "passing hint" was really an intense discussion covering nine short chapters of *The City of God*,[23] and in the second place he overlooks the fact that Augustine credited earlier Romans, including Sallust and Cicero, with similar insights.[24]

According to Augustine, the earliest Romans desired nothing more than the liberty of their city. Once this was achieved, however, they followed their next most intense desire: the desire for glory, which Augustine defines as "the judgment of men when they think well of others."[25] We may call this their second moral period. The astonishing speed and extent of their development in this period were due entirely to their passionate attachment to glory. In Augustine's estimate, this was a vice. However, he agrees with Sallust that it was "a vice closer to a virtue,"[26] for it "checked their other appetites."[27] Now it cannot check the other appetites all by itself. Sallust had argued that without certain "moral qualities," the ambitious man would always try to win glory through "deceit" and the tricks of the canvasser rather than through merit, and here again Augustine agrees.[28] But in the third moral period of Rome, these moral qualities disappeared. Deceitful men, finding the honor they desired always beyond their grasp, became passionately attached to wealth and power instead.[29] These passions Augustine regarded as unmitigated corrupters of morality. They were useless in checking the other appetites; on the contrary, they whipped them on.

Despite the fact that he credits the accomplishments of the Romans to their aptitude for pitting one passion against another, therefore, Augustine does not recommend the device. First, it works only when some of the excellences are already possessed—Sallust's point. Second, it is unstable; it tempts men to the loss of the excellences upon which its success depends. Third, by making men slaves to one of their own passions, it damages their souls. Speaking of glory, Augustine says: "There can be no doubt that it is better to resist this passion than to yield to it. A man is more like God, the purer he is from this contamination. In this life it cannot wholly be rooted out from the heart, because even those souls which are making good progress are not exempt from the temptation. But at least the greed for glory should be overcome by the love of justice; and . . . the love of praise . . . yield place to the love of truth."[30]

"Love," in this passage, means a constant yearning will. Thus the passage has the further merit of reminding us that just as the strategy of pitting passion against passion calls upon the excellences for support, so complete excellence calls upon the passions in a more perfect way. Augustine is often accused of repressive tendencies; the charge has some merit, but it is wholly convincing only when we read him in the context of the twentieth century rather than the fifth. Among other things, the preceding passage is an implicit rebuke to the Stoics and Neoplatonists, who, like the moderns, tended to conceive the "rule of reason" in unrealistically repressive terms. For although I have taken the passage from Book V, in Book XIV Augustine vigorously denies the prevalent beliefs that the passions are always (1) bodily rather than mental in origin, and (2) morbid and inconsistent with a life of tranquil virtue. His claim is that at the proper time, for the right reason, and in the right way, the well-disposed soul will experience not only yearning but also anger, fear, joy, grief, fondness, and even hatred for evil (though this does not mean hatred for individuals, which is inconsistent with Augustine's faith).[31]

Perhaps the first modern to have appreciated the possibilities of fighting fire with fire was Machiavelli. In many respects he was still medieval, and like Augustine he gleaned his insights from Roman history, or so he said. Running through his *Discourses on the First Ten Books of Titus Livius*[32] like a brass thread is the idea that the passion for glory can not only incite acts of benefit to the community but also check the potentially oppressive desire for gain. But at what cost! In Chapters 26 and 27 of Book I, Machiavelli teaches that under a regime organized along these lines, men who wish to be "entirely good" must avoid statecraft altogether, while men who seek glory in the public arena must know how to be "entirely bad": otherwise, "when an evil deed has in itself some grandeur or magnanimity, they will not know how to perform it."[33]

One may wish that besides Livy, Machiavelli had studied Augustine, Sallust, and Cicero; one may even imagine that if he had, his work would have taken a different turn. But he did not find this idea in Livy, either. The mortal wounds of modernity seem to have been inflicted by something more than mistaken generalizations.

Sublimation

Machiavelli was pleased to let out the genie of glory in the expectation that this magical creature would stuff the genie of greed back in. However, it is never safe to assume that a passion out of sight is a passion out of mind; genies have uncanny ways of changing shape and sneaking out of their bottles anyway. In fact, this is the very basis of the third strategy, which is to deny a passion its usual objects so that it *mutates* and fastens onto different objects. Since Nietzsche, we have known this as "sublimation," a term later popularized by Freud. But the idea is very old. Plato, for instance, thought that lovers, tyrants, and philosophers were all driven by the same thing—relentless, mysterious, all-hungry Eros.[34] The reflection influenced his choice of students and led him, as it led Aristotle after him, to prescribe metaphysical contemplation as the only drink heady enough to quench the tyrannical urge[35]—though Plato's experiences with Dionysius the Younger, tyrant of Syracuse, and Aristotle's experiences with Alexander the Great ought to suggest second thoughts.[36] Among the moderns, Rousseau regarded sublimation no less highly. For example, he exploited the phenomenon in his didactic novel, *Emile*, subtitled *On Education*.[37] Emile is raised in such a way that as he enters puberty, the "dark ferment" of his sexual passion is converted into romantic love as well as political idealism.

Exactly what is this strange psychic mutation? Essentially two different kinds of explanations have been offered. The very thoughtlessness of our assent to the term "sublimation" betrays how thoroughly we have accepted one of these explanations and forgotten the other. At the root of the English term is the Latin root *sublimare*, which means to raise or uplift; the idea is that something which is base is *made* sublime, that what is lower is made to evolve into what is higher. In keeping with this, we moderns believe that Eros is "really" nothing but sexual desire. Underneath the fine garments of the most holy aspiration we are always expecting to find a naked body.

The other explanation is radically different. By its lights, Eros is "really" the longing for the Good *as such*, not for any good *thing* but for the divine principle in which every good thing has its source. Although this longing can be attached to other objects— to sex, to power, generally to anything in which we can momentarily forget our finity and isolation—these are actually cases of mistaken identification. Whether Plato accepted the first explanation or the second is not always clear. From his *Republic* one is tempted to reply, "the first"; from his *Symposium*, "the second." For an unambiguous example of the second kind of theorizing we may turn to Charles Williams' interpretation of romantic love, as found in *The Figure of Beatrice*, a study of Dante's *Divine Comedy*. The occasion for this interpretation is Dante's poetic use of a real girl, with whom he had fallen deeply in love, as an epiphany, a showing forth of the Grace of God.

The wise pagan Vergil is able to lead Dante through Hell and Purgatory, but only Beatrice is able to lead him through the realm of Paradise. This could easily have been idolatrous. However, Williams suggests that what the lover beholds in the beloved is never the beloved as she really is but a vision of human nature fresh from the hand of God, untouched by the Fall. The vision is real, and in order to resist its force a man would have to be made of stone. Thus Dante's allegory is vindicated, but on the strict condition that he never confuse the figure of Beatrice with the flesh-and-blood girl—a condition of which Dante himself seemed well aware.

What concerns us here is not love but politics, not romance but a certain kind of idealism. What we want to know is whether the political use of sublimation is appropriate. Now from the point of view of the *second* kind of theory, it looks perilous, because it is an invitation to the very kind of idolatry from which Dante narrowly escaped: the deification not of a girl but of the Leader, the People, or the General Will. However, in the present climate of opinion it may be more profitable to concentrate on the first kind of theory, and that is what I will do.

An assumption common to all theories of the first kind is that arousing a passion—or, following Freud, a "drive"—is very much like pressurizing a tank, while acting out the passion is very much like relieving the pressure. A further assumption is that there are *fewer* tanks than there are passions; it follows that most tanks can be pressurized by more than one passion. Thus if a particular valve on a pressurized tank is out of service, one can just as easily relieve the pressure through another valve. This is "displacement." But if *all* the relief valves are jammed as pressure continues to rise, then the pressure may deform the tank (or, if you prefer, blow it up to its proper shape and dimensions) and leak out from someplace nowhere near any of the valves. This is "sublimation." Frustrate a sexually aroused man, for instance, and he may begin to pick fights with other men—displacement. Now force a vow of celibacy and nonviolence upon him but keep up the sexual arousal. He may take up art and religion, or if he already has them, they may become infused with an erotic glow—sublimation.

It is hard to know whether to classify such explanations under sorcery or hydraulics. It is even harder to know what to make of them. The events they purport to explain are real enough. On the other hand, the explanations proposed do not jibe at all with what little we know about the nervous system. Freud's expectation that some sort of nervous energy or phlogiston answering to his "libido" would eventually be found has been disappointed; in general the nervous system (such parts of it as are understood) seems less and less like a tank, or Freudian "reservoir," and more and more like a computer. Behavioral evidence against these explanations has also been accumulating. For instance, if passions or "drives" really worked as pressurizers, then we should expect that anything which increased pressure in the "tank" would be unpleasant, while anything which diminished the pressure would be pleasant. Yet human beings find arousal as well as consummation pleasant, and generally seem to enjoy their passions. (This is why one of the characters in Plato's *Gorgias* declares that the happy man has not only the means of satisfying his desires but also the means of whipping them up, prompting Socrates' ironic reply that in this case the happiest life would be one of continuous itching and continuous scratching.)[38] Likewise, research with animals has shown that the opportunity to perform nonconsummatory responses can be positively reinforcing—hardly what one would expect if performing them were unpleasant.[39]

Moreover, the events that these explanations concern can often be accounted for in other ways; a "tank" is simply not needed to explain how functionally unrelated behaviors may yet be causally linked. For instance, we saw in the last chapter that apparent instances of "displacement"—that is, seemingly irrelevant behavior in situations of conflict—can be explained as nothing more than the expression of responses low in order of prepotency when the highest-ranked responses are deadlocked. I speculate that apparent instances of sublimation can also be provided with alternative explanations. Delaying sexual gratification in youth does seem to contribute to certain turns of the imagination; but to suggest that, like any other dispositions, these turns of imagination will persist even outside the contexts in which they originate does not require a belief in alchemy.

Banishing the notion of the magical "drive" should also relieve

Christian and secular humanists of a persistent source of embar-
rassment. For years we have been insisting that human beings
have "fewer" drives than animals, or "more" drives than animals, or drives that are "more general" or "more contradictory";
or that unlike animals, human beings can "rise above" their
drives. The truth is more likely that we have no drives and that
the animals haven't any either. We take dispositions for "drives"
because of a massive confusion between typical acquisitions and
innate possessions. The springs of our distinction from animals
lie elsewhere.

But a rose by any other name is just as sweet, and an instance
of "sublimation" by any other name or theory is just as real.
Whether or not we explain the phenomenon with the hindrance
of fictitious tanks and reservoirs, the question remains whether it
is safe to use it for civic purposes—for instance, by making some
kind of connection between sexual passion and political idealism
in young people, as Rousseau proposed.

The analogy we discarded a little while ago merely returns at
this point, for as Rousseau clearly realized, political idealism of
this kind is similar to romantic love. We can gain a purchase on
the answer to our question by developing the parallel. Romantic
love is exciting, tempestuous, and impulsive; while it lasts, it
draws the whole personality into its wind and rain and elec-
tricity. It is unrealistic: on the modern view, what lovers see
when they gaze into each other's eyes is nine-tenths imagination.
It is friendly to reason only so long as reason does not challenge
its illusions. It is utopian, for lovers have no sense of their own
limitations. It can call forth amazing acts of sacrifice, for having
no sense of their own limitations, lovers want to squander themselves on each other. At the same time it is utterly selfish, for in
the first rush of love lovers' ears are filled with din, and even on
the chance that someone else exists, no one else matters. In this
wind the soul is like a sail torn loose in a gale. Romantic love is
capricious, fitful, and unaccountable. We should certainly regard a man or woman who had never loved as incomplete; yet
romantic love is not the whole of love, and by itself it is not an
unmitigated good.

Of the features of romantic love enumerated above, most seem
to sit ill with practical wisdom, and political idealism in young

people has all the features of romantic love with this difference: that the beloved is not a person but something bigger than a person; therefore, its circle of effects is correspondingly greater. As romantic love can develop into mature love, so political idealism can develop into mature idealism; but as romantic love more often turns sour or decays into dependence, youthful idealism more often turns cynical or decays into fanaticism. With a wider circle of effects, this may be a social calamity. I am compelled to conclude that idealism of this kind is not only different from political excellence but an extremely dangerous surrogate for it; it can give height to the aspirations of a young person in whom we have already taken pains to cultivate the excellences, but it will maim him otherwise.

Domestication

The fourth strategy is the only one of the four that is wholly modern. It was not discussed by the classical writers at all, and its introduction into statecraft has changed the face of the world by clearing the way for capitalism and *ragione di stato*. For an account of the controversies from which it finally emerged as a new conventional wisdom, once again there is no better authority than Hirschman. As before, my own brief remarks will be analytical rather than historical in their primary intention.

The fourth device is simply to *domesticate* the passions by converting them into stable and consistent preferences that one seeks to satisfy in a methodical manner. The alleged advantage for statecraft is that passions, by being domesticated, become so regular in their operation that they can be anticipated by the prudent and manipulated by clever institutional arrangements. Our own constitutional system clearly favors this strategy. Although it provides only bulwarks against undomesticated passions—artificial delays in the legislative process, for instance—it puts individual "interests," or domesticated passions, to good use. Thus Madison proclaimed that "ambition must be made to counteract ambition."[40]

Here is how a passion is to be domesticated. First, it is directed to a *particular* external good—not just any external good will do. To begin with, the external good must be a feasible match for the passion in question. In material wealth, the passion of avarice has a match already. But material wealth can also be a match for the passion for admiration, because the signs of wealth impress other people. Adam Smith thought that the feasibility of this match was due to the workings of his all-embracing process, sympathy. Although the enjoyment of wealth tends to wear off, he said, most men do not realize this; consequently, they assume that the wealthy are happy, and they sympathize with this happiness. Ironically, the sympathy itself *does* make the wealthy happy; more precisely, the wealthy sympathize with the good feelings which through a prior act of sympathy men have conceived for them.[41] Having never been in a position to find out, I offer no judgment as to whether this is true.

In the second place, the external good with which the passion is matched must be one that lends itself to methodical acquisition. Thanks to its durability, its fungibility, and all the other qualities that interest economists, material wealth obviously lends itself to methodical acquisition—although we tend to forget that this is only because of the invention of money and banking and all the other instruments and institutions that reduce uncertainty and facilitate credit, saving, investment, and exchange.

Not all passions lend themselves to domestication. This is partly because not all passions can be well matched with external goods, and partly because not all external goods lend themselves in the same degree as wealth to methodical acquisition. So it is that the Arabian Nights quality we have already seen in these strategies deepens. Whereas Machiavelli wanted to let the genie of Glorious Deeds out of his bottle in the expectation that he would stuff the genie of Cupidity back in, later writers proposed to let the genie of Cupidity back out, tame him, rename him Self-Interest, and have him stuff the genie of Glorious Deeds back in. It is interesting to speculate whether other institutions might facilitate the methodical acquisition of other external goods to the same degree to which ours facilitate the methodical acquisition of material wealth.

Now sometimes when a man cannot afford a tune-up, he prevents his auto from stalling by keeping his foot on the gas. Revved up, it runs smoothly, even though its idle is rough. Likewise, slow tops wobble more than fast. The same applies here. For the peculiar thing about a domesticated passion is that it is not, as one would think, the same as a *moderated* passion. In fact, as the "interest" in material wealth demonstrates, it is likely to be insatiable; and since this insatiability is one of the chief contributions to the regularity of its operations, if it is not insatiable already, it must be made so. In ages past, ceaseless stimulation of the public appetites had always been an immediate threat to public order. Under the regime of "interest" it remains a threat in the long run, but in the short run it becomes an absolute requirement.

If the strategy of countervailance could be described as fighting fire with fire, then the strategy of domestication can be described as fighting fuel with fuel. For its means are *nearly* identical to those discussed earlier.

1   Where a domesticated passion is apt to be engaged by an attractive but inappropriate object, distract it with an even more attractive but appropriate object.

Where no appropriate object is more attractive, so contrive matters that the first object cannot be pursued without the *loss* of an *equally* attractive object. This may either

2   immobilize the individual, or

3   clear the way for engagement by a third object—appropriate, attractive, but less attractive than the two objects between which the passion is deadlocked.

But methodically insatiable passion is double edged. Because it is methodical, it can indeed be manipulated by clever institutional arrangements. But because it is insatiable, it always tends to defeat these arrangements before long—to find the loopholes. Therefore, these arrangements must become more and more complicated. The authors of the *Federalist* warned that when the laws of a nation are highly complex and in a constant state of change, eventually only those with the most to gain in circumventing them can afford the effort required to understand them.[42] They did not realize that their dependence upon the fourth strategy made this outcome nearly inevitable. One of the leading ironies of our era is that we think that the proliferation of interests is the greatest source of our political difficulties, while no long ago it was hailed as their most promising solution.

A Retrospective

Is it possible to compromise without being contaminated? Modernity has recognized only one use for the passionate strategies that I have sketched: to escape the demands of a politics of excellence, and build the City on a lower but firmer foundation. Yet we have seen that the lower foundation is not any firmer than the higher. Classical political theory hinted at a better use for the passionate strategies, a use that might be called the "imitation" of excellence.[43] This was the rationale for the "polity," or "mixed" regime, in which, out of regard for the fatality of all ideals, the demands of excellence are moderated—*for the sake of excellence itself*: for excellence provides the standard according to which every compromise is judged, so long as it lasts, and according to which the pathologies implicit in every compromise are battled.[44] Had the classical political theorists explained this concept of imitation more clearly, perhaps the political theorists of modernity would have been less eager to bury them. Unfortunately, their discussion of the polity was so vague that the absolutely fundamental difference between the imitation of excellence and the *abdication* of excellence is overlooked by most readers. Helped along by the modern corruption of the meaning of the term "virtue," we blithely remark Machiavelli's debt to classical republicanism for his theory of the mixed regime, and sometimes even regard our own constitutional system as a polity in the classical sense. Moreover, the classical discussions of education in virtue presupposed ideal rather than "desperate" conditions. Such questions as how to develop the proto-virtues as way stations, without allowing them to become neurotic dead ends, received no attention at all; and although Aristotle is sensitive to the fact that most education in virtue is implicit (acquired through actual experience in the institutions and practices of the community) rather than explicit (acquired through vocal instruction), he says next to nothing about what can be done within the limitations of the mixed and balanced regime, where experience may be defective and instruction must be compensatory. If the resurrection of Nature is to succeed as a political program, the reconstruction of the theory of the polity must be its next task.

I don't attempt that task here. More's the pity, in the next section I describe still another, which is even harder. This has been a little tin of a book, chapters packed in like sardines, and we are down to the last sardine. The best for which I can hope is that it may make someone thirsty; anyhow, sardines are good for catching bigger fish. At any rate my own lines are still out.

The Limits of Politics

The desperation of excellence and the perils of the means proposed for doing without it are like the Scylla and Charybdis of political theory. These have been my subject through this point in the chapter. But should we find a way between the monsters, we are not yet assured a way to harbor, for there are two areas where even the most perfect political excellence can hardly find its bearings: war, and revolution. If the other two problems are like Scylla and Charybdis, these are like the edge of the world. From one point of view they are the most fundamental and revealing political acts; from another they are not political at all. To say that we are by Nature political animals is to say that we are animals who cannot become what we most deeply are outside of communities. But if this is so, then war and revolution are not simply affairs in which the worst of men are set free from their customary restraints (which would be bad enough); to threaten political community means to challenge the natural horizon of excellence, so that even the best of men become prey to subpolitical and transpolitical agitations. This is the *penultimate* problem of political "philosophy" and the *ultimate* problem of political "theory," if the first is understood as reflective and the second as injunctive.

I think it is safe to say that of war and revolution, revolution is the knottier from the standpoint of theory. This is not to deny the unprecedented potential of the modern weapons of war to destroy the human race. Nor is it to deny the immense dilemma they pose by killing on such a massive scale that the distinction between combatants and noncombatants is obliterated. But consider: today, not only armies but also lone terrorists disregard the distinction between combatants and noncombatants, and this has nothing to do with their technology. If we could come to a moral understanding of revolution, we could probably come to a moral understanding of war; the reverse is not true. In war, at least, different political communities confront one another as units. Each remains the natural horizon of reference for its own members. In revolution even that horizon is denied, and the revolutionaries attempt to find another.

Now I would like to be my own critic and call attention to the last remark. It had two parts: first, that revolutionaries deny a natural horizon of reference, and second, that in revolution they attempt to find another. By taking these one at a time we may divide our difficulties, even if we cannot resolve them.

In the first part of the remark, the term "deny" is ambiguous. This ambiguity is deliberate. Revolutionaries might either *reject* a natural horizon of reference or *deny that it is natural*, deny that the particular horizon in question is one against which they can reasonably develop their characteristically human powers. This difference is at the root of the distinction John Locke made in 1688 between "rebellion," which he said is always wrong, and "revolution," which he said is always right.[45] Some such distinction seems essential to the matter at hand, and fortunately, the distinction can be extricated from the claims about "Natural Rights" with which Locke mixed it up.

The second part of the remark is more vexing. How far may revolutionaries go in reformulating their horizon? Locke claimed that they may dissolve the government, but that they may not dissolve the *condition* of political community itself. The distinction that this maxim presupposes is not as straightforward as the other one. Granted that political community is more, much more, than government, still—short of a bloodless *coup*—it is hard to see how one can dissolve a government while leaving the political community untouched. In fact, even a bloodless *coup* may not turn the trick. Revolutions are not surgical. Far easier is it to see how one might destroy the political community while leaving the *government* untouched.

Locke's intuitions about the limits of revolution must somehow be disentangled from his unreasonably sharp distinction between government and political community. I am not certain how to do this, but we may be able to develop a feeling for it by glancing at a theory that respects no such limits. One will think that I mean totalitarianism. But good liberals (who will constitute most of my audience) should need no preaching about that—if they do, my cause is lost anyway. I mean Machiavellism. Among my well-mannered students, Machiavelli produces a thrill as much as a shock; *not* to be shocked, I suspect, seems to them a sign of moral courage. They love the "realism" of Machiavelli's lean and muscular prose. He gives profound and articulate expression to the need our political culture gives them to think that they can "take man as he really is," and they are honestly startled when I point out that the founding of Machiavelli's republic is every bit as heroically implausible as the founding of Socrates'. Let us think about this.

When Socrates outlined the ideal regime, he spoke as though human agency were irrelevant to its realization. But something more than absence of mind held him from speaking of how to get from *here* to *there*. As admitted earlier, every existing regime is rooted in interests that are narrower than the comprehensive human good and dispositions that are lower than the excellences. Therefore, in the inception of the regime of the good and the excellent, the ruler would be unable to call upon any of these lesser interests or dispositions for support. In fact, he would have to use human beings like clay—crush them, knead them, remold them, evacuate the city of anyone beyond the age of ten and therefore too old to reshape.[46] Such a ruler would require extraordinary abilities—excellences, if you will—but they would not be comprehended within *political* excellence, because he would have to stand above the city like a god. Nothing in our political experience gives us any understanding of this unpolitical, not to say inhuman, kind of excellence, and in the end Socrates admits that the ideal regime must be founded in the soul rather than in the world at large. In this he was supremely "realistic"; until Machiavelli, who railed against those who found imaginary regimes,[47] his realism stood.

Something in our experience *does* give us insight into the excellence of the state-founder, Machiavelli said: the record of previous successful inceptions of states. From his study of the past, he too concluded that the founder must make all institutions anew; and he drew the further conclusion that for this task, courage and prudence are the sum of virtue, but moderation and justice are the sum of vice.[48] The founder would need nothing in him of a god, but something in him of both man and beast. Thus Machiavelli compares him to Chiron, a centaur and the legendary teacher of Achilles, the hero of the *Iliad*.[49] But if Chiron instructed Achilles, then whom does the founder instruct? He instructs those who are to live in the regime that he founds. His instruction is to be embodied in the institutions that he gives them.[50] *Their* excellence will be quite different from his. This is clear from a contrast of the uses of the term "virtue" in Machiavelli's *Discourses* with the uses of the same term in his *Prince*: theirs will be political; his is outside politics.

And there is the crux of the problem. Machiavelli supposes that a man who *necessarily* lacks political excellence is the best suited to teach it to others. That so many of the ancient figures whom he commends as examples are mythical, like Romulus, while he mythicizes the rest, is very revealing. He justifies the ploy on the grounds that if, when we try to follow these examples, our "virtue" does not come up to theirs, at least it will have "the smell of it."[51] This is presumably to say the smell of a myth. Machiavelli called for a man who would be to all intents and purposes a superior barbarian, but there are no barbarians who are superior. This is what we call his "realism"; for this, he has been called the founder of modern political science.[52]

So there was a point after all in the reticence of the classical thinkers to speak of the path from *here* to *there*. *There*, of course, political science—properly so called—would lose its point. Human purposes would no longer be skewed and scrambled and in need of professional interpretation. *Here* all of our purposes are compromised, all of our regimes are compromises. The concern of students of politics should be to distinguish right compromise from wrong compromise, to expand the possibilities of right compromise, and to learn to think even of war and revolution as means of restoring lost possibilities of compromise. My aim in these remarks has been to speak about theory, rather than theorizing, but I cannot forbear ending with the proposition that as political animals, when we cease to be political we are animals alone.

Nature Questioned

With the Epilogue, this examination of human nature and politics draws to a close. The deepest impulses in human nature point beyond it; the last task of natural philosophy is to come to terms with this fact.

The Critique of Nature

Aristotle said that there are things higher than human beings, yet that in some way the human good concerns them. Modern writers disagree; to the extent that they speak of a human good at all, they make it out as a pleasing pattern of partial goods, all within the human circuit. But no matter how elegantly we are addressed about plans and narratives, something warns us not to buy that. Why?

The author or authors of the Book of Ecclesiastes even say that joy itself is vexation of spirit; that everything mere Nature understands as good and flourishing—even purpose, even self-knowledge—is empty in the end. Indeed the most baffling impulse in human nature is the one that demands a *critique* of Nature—the one that makes us feel the form of our existence as an enclosure—that moves us to leave all human perspectives behind despite the sometime suspicion that individual existence *is* perspective, and nothing more—that makes us unwilling to take our purposes at face value so that we are always looking beyond or beneath them, heedless of the voids we know good and well may await us there. This impulse is characteristic, not innate. That is to say, it must be learned, although in natural settings it is almost inevitably learned. Since it must be learned, it is not equally strong in everyone and even passes without notice in many of us; again, since it must be learned, it takes different forms. The last task of natural philosophy, as of all human endeavor, is to come to terms with it: to find a way to reach past ourselves without turning against ourselves, to look beyond or beneath human perspectives without feeling contempt or indifference for them. Therefore, the last excellence of human beings, not least the attempters of philosophy, is the one that equips them for this calling. It is neither an integral, nor an intimate, nor a practical, nor a political excellence. We must have it, because without it all of these other dimensions of excellence are imperiled.

The longing that we must consider expresses itself sometimes in a pursuit of origins and sometimes in a pursuit of purposes, of ends. Its vehicles include certain kinds of science and history, although it is not the same as curiosity, and certain kinds of metaphysics and religion, although it is not the same as a merely social piety. The purest and most revealing examples of this longing, *uncontrolled* by the critical virtue it requires, are at opposite ends of the spectrum: Socrates, and Nietzsche. Socrates was so heedless in the pursuit of last things that he allowed himself to be needlessly destroyed by his countrymen. Nietzsche was so consumed by the pursuit of first things that he destroyed himself.

As depicted by Plato, Socrates believed that Nature at large, or Being, is fundamentally coherent, and that this coherence is divine. But the truest part of the soul is not strictly human; it is divine (he thought) in the same way. Therefore the highest good of a human being is to escape the "cave" of conventional understanding in order to gaze with the eye of the soul upon the "sun" of Being. This escape is in the deepest way problematic. When he first emerges from the cave, the philosopher is blinded because he is unaccustomed to the light of truth. When he returns to the cave, he is again blinded because he is no longer used to the dark of opinion. Other men find him a fool when he tries to explain that the flickering shadows on the walls of the cave are not real beings; he cannot teach them the truth and is reduced to teaching them a more salutary opinion than the opinions they already hold.[1]

There is an even deeper problem that Socrates did not state plainly. The eye of the *body* cannot gaze upon the sun of the *heavens*: in the attempt it will simply be burned. Then how can the eye of the *soul* gaze upon the sun of *Being*? In the attempt it should be burned, too. Something like this seems to have happened to Socrates. To his last day he insisted that he was ignorant of the things he exhorted the most promising youths of Athens to know. When a young friend eagerly demanded an account of the world outside the cave, Socrates wistfully replied that the fellow could not understand it, and that he could not provide it.[2]

Of course, Socrates could return to the cave, but having learned that the things within it are shadows, how could he take them seriously any longer? He included the human things among the first objects of knowledge, but not of devotion.[3] This calls to mind several aspects of his personal life. Socrates was a cold husband, as we see from his indifference to the grief of his wife when he was about to die.[4] He was an undependable father, who spent great amounts of time with all the beautiful youths of the upper classes but not with his own sons.[5] On the report of one of the characters in Plato's *Symposium*, he was the kind of lover who allows himself to become the object of lust that he refuses to satisfy.[6] Though he had profound insight into politics, he was a poor citizen who did not even know the rules of procedure in the public assembly.[7] He understood philosophical friendship, but no other kind, for he deserted his friends in the end; going against their pleas, at his trial he wasted the opportunity to explain his vocation, insulted the jury, and practically asked to be put to death.[8] Philosophy, he said, is learning how to die[9]—not learning to live, as one might have thought—and he went out chattering.

Religious souls are not surprised by any of this. They understand Socrates' longing, but reject his pride in human intellect. If the vision of God is to illuminate instead of burn, they say, it must be provided by divine Grace. No doubt they are right, but as an affair of *knowledge*, this does not make the vision any less problematic. By Grace, Dante said, he experienced the vision of God; but after relapsing into his ordinary powers he could no longer understand it and was left with only the memory of Love and the pain of separation.[10] After his vision, this political exile was no less alienated from human things than before—more, perhaps, because now he realized why they cannot satisfy.

As for the one who *still* insists on answers—what does he do while he is awaiting them? Pascal felt the pain of separation *without* the comfort of a memory:

> When I see the blindness and the wretchedness of man, when I regard the whole silent universe, and man without light, left to himself, and, as it were, lost in this corner of the universe, without knowing who has put him there, what he has come to do, what will become of him at death, and incapable of all knowledge, I become terrified, like a man who should be carried off in his sleep to a dreadful desert island, and should be awakened without knowing where he is, and without means of escape. And thereupon these wretched and lost beings, having looked around them, and seen some pleasing objects, have given and attached themselves to them. For my own part, I have not been able to attach myself to them.[11]

So misery, despair, longing, and contempt glitter together like the fragments of broken flasks: supreme passion flows together with the most wretched indifference, like wine mingled with gall. From this there grows a suspicion that Socrates made two errors, not one only, and that the second is perpetuated even here. The pride in his own powers that made him try to find the Absolute instead of letting it find him—Dante and Pascal have exposed this error, but it was only the first. To regard reconciliation as an affair of *knowledge* rather than *relationship*, of *answers* rather than *trust*—this error, persisting, turns the fruit of life as bitter as the worm.

All of this will seem very strange to modern ears. The longing for last things has been pretty well drummed out of us. Nietzsche called it "sick"; Freud called it "neurotic"; and we were the first apostles of what William James called the "religion of healthy-mindedness."[12] Philosophy in the meantime has been made an academic specialty and a footnote to other academic specialties. What professors do concerns tenure, not salvation, and if perchance they *do* become indifferent to human things, nobody gives a damn anyway; they aren't apt to corrupt the youth. Or at least that is what we think.

Nothing is permanent in the human circuit; this will change, as it has changed before. But even as it stands, it is only half the story. The spirituality of modernity, such as it is, is found within science and history, not within metaphysics and religion. Our longing is to know first things, not last things; for the question, "Why are we here?" can be taken in two senses, as meaning either "What do we come from?" or as meaning "What are we here for?" and we act as though an answer to the first can double for the second. It *can't*—although it can evoke some of the same deep emotions. Thus instead of trying to place human purposes in a scheme that is both higher and bigger, we try to place them within a scheme that is lower, but still bigger. We see them as *caused* rather than as *intended*, whether the system of causation we have in mind is biological, psychological, cultural, historical, linguistic, or a melange of all of these. This way of thinking is highly but subtly corrosive.

In saying this I do not mean to suggest that purposes are *not* both caused, and causes; clearly, they are, even when they are caused only by *reasons*. But just as the notion of "free will" can make us forget that purposes are caused, so the desire to "explain" them makes us forget that purposes are causes. In fact, the second kind of forgetfulness is more dangerous than the first. For a belief in free will to sap the meaning from life is unusual; on the contrary, it encourages the ordinary individual to take responsibility for his actions, and it encourages the scholar to take the truth claims of different systems of thought very seriously indeed. By contrast, when ordinary individuals get into the habit of regarding their aspirations as byproducts of their genes, or their times, or their social classes, or their childhood experiences—or some combination of such things—they are likely to think either that there is no point in aspiring, or that it does not matter to what they aspire; and when *scholars* get into the habit of regarding the aspirations of *other* people in this way (for they almost always exclude themselves), they are likely to develop a sort of humane cynicism according to which every culture is permitted its own system of thought and value, each of them is wrong, and none of them is to blame. Therefore, not only can the quest for first things evoke some of the same deep emotions as the quest for last things, as we saw before, but it also poses much the same peril—whether deeply emotional or not.

Nietzsche—perhaps history's most zealous warrior against last things, self-proclaimed Odysseus of first things, the original "genealogist of morals"[13] and the inventor of "philosophizing with a hammer"[14]—was also among the first to realize this. He called himself the first European nihilist, and the first European to overcome nihilism.[15] He believed that the rest of Europe would take another two centuries—first to realize that God is dead,[16] and then to realize that in order *not* to will to follow Him, man would have to seize His prerogatives—in ontology, or the shape of reality, no less than in deontology, or morals. Many thinkers before Nietzsche had asked, "What must the world be like if there is no God?" Nietzsche asked, "What must the world be like for me to *be God*?"

What this had to do with the quest for first things he made clear with a metaphor that reversed the Socratic parable of the cave. Instead of saying that he wanted to emerge into the light to gaze at the sun, he said that he wanted to go *deeper* into the labyrinth, like Theseus underneath the Palace of Knossos—presumably in order to slay the "all-too-human" beast he expected to find there.[17] The surface meaning of this figure is that Nietzsche proposed severing the Socratic quest for self-knowledge from the Socratic quest for divine harmony. This set the stage for the psychoanalytic movement that followed in the twentieth century. However, the figure's darker overtones set the stage for darker things as well. This brings me to another point of resemblance between the maldeveloped longing for first things and the maldeveloped longing for last things—and between Nietzsche and Socrates.

The one case in which a maldeveloped devotion to first or to last things does *not* produce indifference to human things is when their respective spheres of aspiration—the transpolitical, and the political—are merged. For although the visionary cannot transmit his vision to others, he can make them live by it; although he cannot be devoted to their rule, he can rule. Indeed,

Socrates intimates that the philosopher is a poor citizen in every regime *except* the one in which he rules; and Nietzsche intimates the same thing about the "overman." For Socrates, of course, the philosopher is nothing but the heroic seeker of last things, just as for Nietzsche the overman is nothing but the heroic seeker of first things. In this respect the only difference between them is that the philosopher "imitates" the divine vision while the overman "creates" it—or what passes for it.

This may seem pure fantasy, but history provides abundant grounds for the suspicion that anything that can be conceived can be an object of aspiration. The remarks of Socrates that the intervention of a god would be necessary to bring the rule of the wise into existence[18] were probably meant merely to point up the infinitesimal likelihood of the event—but they can also be taken literally. For instance, some of the Islamic Platonists of the Middle Ages identified Socrates' philosopher-kings with the Prophet and his successors, on whose behalf, they believed, God *had* intervened. Thus al-Farabi: "So let it be clear to you that the idea of the Philosopher, Supreme Ruler, Prince, Legislator, and Imam is but a single idea."[19] For an example nearer to home, consider Hegel's doctrine of last things instead of Socrates'. Hegel said nothing about philosopher-kings. But by adapting Hegel's doctrine to the needs of revolutionary justification, by changing History from something that is at every moment complete (as Hegel thought) into something that at every moment demands completion, Marx too showed a way to fuse the political and transpolitical spheres of aspiration.

Socrates did not anticipate the religious and ideological misappropriation of philosophical doctrines, because he underestimated the dreadful power of philosophical impulses in unphilosophical men. The same cannot be said of Nietzsche; fully aware of the dreadful power of *creative* impulses in *uncreative* men (and in the strictest sense of the term, does that not include all of us?), he wrote about it at length, and in many places, under the rublic of "resentment." He even spoke of his "terrible fear" that the creators whose coming he proclaimed would "turn out badly."[20] Yet in the end the dreadful power overcame him too, and he exclaimed, "Let everything perish that cannot stand *our* truths!"[21] Everything nearly did, in Europe, when the Nazis came to power.

The voice in us which cries out that there must be more than human nature will not be denied, should not be denied; it is the very impulse that made us aware of the difference between Nature and Custom in the first place. Yet we must deny it the terrible pleasure of turning against the Nature from which it springs. Our desperate arcs beyond and behind ourselves must always be moderated by Trust; and they must always return trustingly to their starting point. By no other means can the last human excellence be cultivated, and by no other means can those whose ears are filled with siren songs be saved. To say something about it is is the final purpose of this book and, if I may say so, a personal as well as a philosophical duty. There is indeed a cave; but Socrates and Nietzsche were both, I believe, mistaken about its configuration. It will be my duty to correct them.

The Snares of the Wise

Socrates believed that we sit, shackled, deep within the cave, facing the back wall. Immediately behind us a fire furnishes flickering artificial light. Although the mouth of the cave is too far behind us for us to receive its illumination, once we are unshackled and turned around, it is not a long walk.

This is false. In the first place, the cave is not at the end of a horizontal tunnel, but at the base of a volcanic chimney; it is more a cavern than a cave. The floor of the cave, in turn, is not flat, but an irregularly shaped hill; terraces hewn by human labor are placed here and there at different elevations down the slope. We live unshackled, on these terraces. A diffuse light floods the cave; standing at the apex of the hill, immediately beneath the chimney, the eye seeks its source but is hindered by the intervening mists. Nothing can be perceived but a vague brightening, occasionally shot through by thin pure rays. All around the base of the hill is a thicket; beyond it, tunnels lead off into solid volcanic rock in all directions.

The cave is large, so large that although we are free to move around in it, many of us never realize that it is a cave at all. It is not an unpleasant place, and at times it is a place of great loveliness, except at night when marauders trample the crops and ruin the terraces. However, the days are long, and full of color and growing things.

Among those who know the cave for what it is, some have tried to leave—quite a few of them over the years, though never many at one time. Sometimes others have tried to prevent them from leaving, but usually they have found a way. Some have come back. Some have been brought back. Others have disappeared.

There have been four kinds of travelers. First of all, there have been men and women who climbed to the apex of the hill floor, stretched their arms upward and jumped—or simply stretched even further. Some of these have exhausted themselves and collapsed. Others have given up and made their way down to the terraces again. Still others have sat down in frustration and waited, refusing to leave. If their friends brought them food, they ate; if they had no friends, they starved.

Men and women of the second kind, with the same intention of ascending the chimney, have begun differently. Instead of climbing to the apex of the hill, they have descended to its base and tried to make their way up the inner walls, hanging upside down like wingless moths. Among those who have not fallen or leaped to their ends, some have returned the way they came; a few have not. None of those who have returned had reached the top of the chimney. A few claimed to have done so, but they were later shown to have lied or deceived themselves. Some one or two of those who have not returned have been accounted for in a way that permits us to guess at the fates of the others, for according to reports, there are niches cut by hand tools at various altitudes up the chimney. In some of these, human remains have been discovered. Even a few living souls have been found in them: some have been content where they were; other poor wretches have wanted to return but feared to make the attempt because they had gone blind in the glare, and the travelers have had to leave them behind. Some of the niches are very large and very empty. Attempts have even been made to pull entire villages up to the niches by ropes and pulleys, whether they wanted to go or not.

Men and women in the third group have not tried to ascend the chimney at all, reasoning that an alternative path to the surface might be threaded through the labyrinth of tunnels leading from the base of the hill. Unfortunately these connect, divide, and intersect like nylon mesh, and a great many of the intrepid have simply got lost. Some of the tunnels do seem to lead upward for a while but then turn downward without warning; others begin with a steep downward slope but eventually begin to rise; most end in cul-de-sacs; a few lead to caverns at deeper levels. Reports of these caverns that filter back read much like edge-of-the-world stories brought back by ancient mariners and are probably not to be trusted—reports, for example, of Minotaurs, and of eyeless men who live in perpetual darkness, play at dice, and talk with the Minotaurs about philosophy. These can be read about in old manuscripts, and have been painted quite recently. At any rate, the subterranean caverns are known to be the source of the marauding bands that emerge into our own cavern during the nights, which fall at irregular intervals.

The best-known explorer of the labyrinth, whom I have already mentioned, did not enter it by design. Rather he was chased into it by wild animals when, in attempting to find a way to ascend the hill, he got lost in the thicket at its base. After this, he was fortunate enough to find a humane guide, who has since disappeared. According to our traveler, at the greatest depth in the labyrinth is a vast lake of ice in which are frozen the bodies of previous travelers. On the other side of this lake, he says, is another tunnel, which can be reached only by crossing the ice, and that leads all the way to the surface of the earth, beloved of the sun. Many doubt his veracity, however, because there is so little that he can say about the light that bathed him there.

A fourth group of men and women has insisted that the diffuse light up the chimney is nothing but the highest reflection of fires burning in the cave itself; many believe this, but these men and women have distinguished themselves by entering the labyrinth without any intention of reaching the earth's surface. Some of them have even thought that there is no such thing as a surface—that all the universe is rock and cave and tunnel. Few of these have ever returned. There are stories that some have become eyeless men and preachers to the marauders. One was found where he had fallen on his way, not really far into the labyrinth at all, although he seemed to think that he had gone much farther; he was quite alive, but hardly aware, and murmured continually about following Ariadne's thread, although there was no thread nearby. An old friend, who cared little for tunnels, entered them for the sake of retrieving him, and gave him into the care of his sister, who nursed him until he died. She also took photographs of him and allowed him, in this state, to be made the object of a cult.

The more successful travelers—that is to say, those who have returned to their friends and loved ones alive—have occasionally brought geological observations from the tunnels, and contour maps of the hill drawn from the perspective of the chimney. These have chiefly been useful in planning new terraces in the hill, as well as fortifications for use at night. But the loveliness of the cavern is due to the light alone. Just at this moment, in a parting of the mists between the beats of my heart, everything in it seemed to glow from behind.

Notes

PROLOGUE: *The Burial of Nature*

1. *New Organon.*
2. For an excellent introduction to the field, see Robert A. Hinde, *Animal Behavior: A Synthesis of Ethology and Comparative Psychology*, to which I will have several occasions to refer in the course of this book.
3. See esp. his *On Human Nature*, the companion volume to *Sociobiology: The New Synthesis.*
4. For discussion of this and other errors of sociobiology—especially its flawed assumptions and persistent abuse of empirical method—see for instance Ashley Montagu, ed., *Sociobiology Examined.* Quite a bit of other material bearing on the issue of sociobiology, and on ethology generally, is listed in my bibliography.
5. The verb is *phusein.* For more about this, see the Preface to Joseph Cropsey and Leo Strauss, eds., *History of Political Philosophy.*
6. This much is clear in the formal charges brought against Socrates, whom most Athenians regarded as just another natural philosopher. See Plato's *Apology* for an account of the trial.
7. The play, of course, is *The Clouds.* Besides being funny, brilliant, and flamboyantly irresponsible for its misrepresentation of Socrates, *The Clouds* is one of the best surviving documents on the reaction of Athenian conservatives to Sophism. See esp. the cockfight between the "Just Speech" and the "Unjust Speech."
8. See esp. Plato's *Gorgias*, which records Socrates' conversation with a teacher of rhetoric of that name.
9. These themes preoccupy the characters in Plato's *Republic.*
10. These are primary subjects of Aristotle's *Politics* and secondary

187

subjects of his *Nicomachean Ethics* (named for his son, Nicomachus, and hereafter to be called the *Ethics*).

CHAPTER ONE: *The Resurrection of Nature*

1. This passage is from Bk. III, Pt. I, Sec. I, and may be found in the Hume anthology listed in the bibliography.

2. Moore's argument can be found in a book entitled *Principia Ethica*, which is Latin for "principles of ethics": an affectation, of course, since the book is written in English.

3. See esp. the physics of human passions advanced in Pt. I, entitled "Of Man."

4. This is the theory of the "covenant," or Social Contract.

5. Jeremy Bentham, the principal founder of utilitarianism, is notorious for saying in his *Introduction to the Principles of Morals and Legislation* that so far as pleasure is concerned, "pushpin is as good as poetry." Pushpin is, or was, a game similar to bowling. Concerning the principle of "neutrality," see Bruce Ackerman, *Social Justice in the Liberal State*, and Ronald Dworkin, "Liberalism." In Ackerman's version, neutralism is the doctrine that every notion of a full and good life is just as good as every other, and that it is illiberal to say otherwise. This doctrine is supposed to serve as a constraint in quarrels over who gets what piece when the social pie is cut—which, so far as Ackerman is concerned, is the sum and substance of political discourse: "power," so-called.

6. This is found in *The Gay Science*, Bk. 4, Sec. 290. The title is an allusion to *la gaya scienza* of the Provençal poets.

7. See his *Beyond Good and Evil*, Pt. V, Sec. 188.

8. The most important sources for these views are Kant's *Critique of Practical Reason* and *Groundwork for the Metaphysics of Morals*.

9. This passage is from *The Prince*, Ch. XVII.

10. Genesis 3:6.

11. The utter depravity of this dead Nature is most vigorously argued by John Calvin. Martin Luther comes in a close second.

12. For Rousseau's account of the degeneration of primal man, I am relying on his *Discourse on the Origin and Foundations of Inequality among Men*, also known as his "second" discourse. However, the paradoxical remarks about the fate of social man that Rousseau offers at the very end of this discourse must be augmented by his doctrine of the General Will, found in *On the Social Contract* and the Geneva manuscript on political economy, among other places.

13. The discussion of the "realm of necessity" and the "realm of

freedom" can be found in *Capital*, Vol. III, Ch. XLVIII. See also a much earlier manuscript entitled "Alienated Labor."

14. This passage and the one preceding it can both be found in the English translation of the book, published in 1969 by Basic Books.

15. Interesting reflections on these themes can be found in Amelie Rorty, ed., *Explaining Emotions*.

16. See *Republic* 352 and 353, where Socrates suggests that just as "there is some work that belongs to a horse," "that which one can only do with it, or best with it," by the same token "there is some work of a soul that you couldn't ever accomplish with any other thing that is."

17. This is from *Ethics* 1098.

18. See his *Love's Body*.

19. *Summa Theologica* I–II, Question 91, Article 6, and Question 82, Articles 1, 2.

20. The translation is Walter Kaufmann's.

CHAPTER TWO: *The Unity of Nature (1)*

1. For a brief account of Thomas' views on time, aeviternity, and eternity, see *Summa Theologica* I, Question 10, especially Articles 4–6. Lengthier speculations on the angelic attributes can be found in his *Treatise on the Angels*, which comprises *Summa Theologica* I, Questions 50–64.

2. All page references given in discussing Rawls in this chapter are to this work.

3. All page references given in discussing MacIntyre later in this chapter are to this work.

4. MacIntyre, 191, 199, 200, 202–3.

5. Ibid., 192 (emphasis mine).

6. Ibid.

7. Ibid., 193.

8. Ibid., 192. MacIntyre says that it may be an institution, a practice, or "a milieu of some other human kind."

9. Ibid., 194.

10. Ibid., 192.

11. Ibid., 194, 196, 197.

12. Ibid., 197, 198. He could easily have said that stories are lived and told simultaneously, as part of the same process—which is nearer the position I adopt later.

13. Ibid., 201.

14. Ibid., 200, 201, 203.

15. Rawls, 408.
16. Ibid., 92, 93.
17. Ibid., 409.
18. Ibid., 416.
19. Ibid., 418.
20. Ibid., 413.
21. Ibid., 410–11.
22. Ibid., 415.
23. Ibid., 416.
24. Ibid., 409, 416.
25. Ibid., 412–14. Rawls applies this principle to short-term plans, then argues that it applies to life-plans as well.
26. Ibid., 412.
27. Ibid., 408, 416–24. Why Rawls believes that desires but not satisfactions are comparable in intensity is a mystery.
28. Ibid., 417–21.
29. This theorem was proven by Türing, and is closely related to Gödel's incompleteness theorems. It may be said that man is not a computational device, but if Rawlsian man differs from one at all, it is not clear how.
30. Rawls, 420–21.
31. Ibid.; see also pp. 293–94.
32. MacIntyre, 152, 183. Cf. Hannah Arendt, who also affirms that life is narrative but also denies that this concerns human nature (*The Human Condition*, 161–67).
33. Ibid., 204, 207.
34. Discussion of this and related matters can be found in Robert A. Hinde, *Animal Behavior*.
35. Nietzsche gives this example in several places; one of them is *The Will to Power*, Bk. III, Sec. 699.
36. This is a basic *motif* of both *The Gay Science* and *Beyond Good and Evil*. A short discussion of the idea is found in his "On Truth and Lie in an Extra-Moral Sense," part of which can be found in Walter Kaufmann, trans., *The Portable Nietzsche*.
37. The basic text for this is *Beyond Good and Evil*, Pt. VII, Sec. 229, where Nietzsche asks us to "consider that even the seeker after knowledge forces his spirit to recognize things against the inclination of his spirit, and often enough against the wishes of his heart—by way of saying No where he would like to say Yes, love, and adore—and thus acts as an artist and transfigurer of cruelty. Indeed, any insistence on profundity and thoroughness is a violation, a desire to hurt the basic

will of the spirit which unceasingly strives for the apparent and the superficial—in all desire to know there is a drop of cruelty." As usual, Nietzsche here begins with a truth (in this case that truth *may* be painful), subtly misstates it, turns it into a half-truth, and finally utters a lie (that without a degree of masochism there is no truth). Elsewhere in *Beyond Good and Evil* he makes it abundantly (if only implicitly) clear that the more something hurts, the more truth he thinks it contains.

38. This is found in his *Case for Christianity*. Cf. St. Paul, who says in Romans 8:18–23 that in the *parousia*, the entire physical creation will share in the redemption of the people of God.

39. See his *Physics*.

40. Thomas takes this for granted in his *Summa Theologica*.

41. Concerning the main point of this chapter: as the Second Person of the Trinity, Christ is called the eternal *logos* (King James Version: "the Word"), which in Greek can mean either "reason" or "speech." But when we describe God as the Author of Nature and History, we have in mind not so much bare abstract intelligence as an infinitely wise and truthful storyteller. That the rational unity of a whole life is the unity of a true story—is it too much to wonder whether this might be some small part of what it means to say that we are "made in His image"?

CHAPTER THREE: *The Unity of Nature (2)*

1. *Republic* 436–39.

2. The principle is invoked in *Republic* 436. According to Allan Bloom's commentary, this is its first known use in philosophy.

3. The idea of comparing the soul with the City is first broached in *Republic* 368–69. By 442 the analogy is complete.

4. The following discussion offers a number of quotations from Hume. All are taken from the same two portions of his *Treatise of Human Nature*—Bk. II, Sec. V; Bk. III, Pt. I, Sec. I—which cover much the same ground in different ways. Page numbers refer to the Hafner anthology, which is listed in my bibliography. This passage is found on p. 23.

5. Ibid.

6. Ibid., 33.

7. Ibid., 34. The verb "prompting" and the adjective "mediate" are from p. 37.

8. Ibid., 25.

9. More precisely, Plato offers the metaphor of a charioteer with a

team of two horses. The charioteer is reason; the horses are spiritedness and desire. This can be found in *Phaedrus*, 246 and 253–55. But Sigmund Freud, in *New Introductory Lectures on Psychoanalysis*, Lecture XXXI, "The Dissection of the Psychical Personality," suggests that "the ego's relation to the id might be compared with that of a rider to his horse. The horse supplies the locomotive energy, while the rider has the privilege of deciding on the goal and of guiding the powerful animal's movement." Freud's debt to Plato has often been remarked.

10. The article is "K-lines: A Theory of Memory," published in *Cognitive Science*.

11. *A Theory of Justice*, 192.

12. See his *Reason and Human Good in Aristotle*.

13. *The Prince*, Ch. XVIII.

14. Needless to say, it primes them differently depending upon whether or not the fetus is counted among the "affected parties"; but what is at stake there is *whether* imagination and sympathy extend to the unborn child, not *how*. Therefore, although this secondary priming is analogous to the focusing role played by the minor premise in a practical syllogism, the analogy is not strict; consequently, we still cannot regard what is going on as a species of deduction. See also my later remarks on Thomas Aquinas.

15. Just as I am classifying meta-ethical positions in order to explore the problem of the rational unity of motive, so Fishkin classifies them in order to explore the problem of moral "subjectivism." Since the underlying principle of his classification is different from the underlying principle of mine, it should come as no surprise that the two classifications come out differently. However, they intersect at two points. What I call "absolutism" corresponds closely with what Fishkin calls "absolutism." Skipping an intervening category that he calls "rigorism," what I call "contra-absolutism" corresponds closely with what he calls "minimal objectivism." Our remaining categories bear no straightforward relation to one another. I should add that probably no stronger argument for a contra-absolutist variety of liberalism can be constructed than Fishkin's. His arguments are presented in detail in *Beyond Subjective Morality* and, more briefly, in "Liberal Theory and the Problem of Justification."

16. This debate occupies the central position in his *Freedom and Reason*.

17. The passage is taken from *Eichmann in Jerusalem*, 135–36.

18. Ibid., 136.

19. Personal communication, cited by permission.

20. Fishkin offers the distinction that this term presupposes on pp. 106–7 of *Beyond Subjective Morality*: "Let us distinguish, broadly, between arguments for a particular moral position that are *internal*, in the sense that they depend on a characterization of morality or the moral point of view itself, and those that are *external*, in that they depend on propositions that are not part of the characterization of morality or the moral point of view, but rather, turn on other claims—for example, claims about God or the structure of the universe or human destiny." For my argument, what is decisive is that Fishkin would regard the facts of human nature as "external" to the moral point of view.

21. The example of Iran is drawn from personal communication and cited by permission. To his great credit, Fishkin clearly discerns the cultural revolution that abstinence from external considerations would require. Because of the inevitable inconclusiveness of all moral reasoning that depends only on internal considerations, members of the culture would have to *stop wanting* conclusiveness. Should they be unable to do this, liberalism would "self-destruct," after which, Fishkin believes, nothing but "subjectivism" would remain. (Here I disagree, as the next paragraph in the text will make clear.) "While I have not shown how subjectivism *must* be avoided," Fishkin concludes on the final page of *Beyond Subjective Morality*, "I have shown how it *may* be, if only we choose to think and to live in the manner required."

22. See *Ethics* 1098.

23. Leviticus 19:18; Matthew 22:39; Mark 12:31; Luke 10:27. The other commandment mentioned in this context is to "love the Lord thy God with all thy heart, and with all thy soul, and with all thy mind." This too has its origin in the Old Testament; see Deuteronomy 6:5.

24. Dante regarded it as the root of the moral crisis from which he escaped in the *Divine Comedy*.

25. This admission is found in *Republic* 487. When Adeimantus complains that of those who linger in the study of philosophy, the majority become wicked while the excellent few become useless, Plato has Socrates happily agree. There follows a lengthy discussion of the reason for this, the gist being that philosophers are liberated from Custom without being able to follow the Truth.

26. I agree with Plato that by and large we are much better at recognizing virtue than at practicing it. But things could be worse: we could be as poor at recognition as we are at practice. See *Laws* 950.

27. *Leviathan*.

28. See his *Treatise on Law* (*Summa Theologica* I–II, Questions 90–114), Question 94, Article 2.

29. The view from which I am distinguishing mine is closely associated with John Searle.

30. See the discussion of "practical" wisdom in the next chapter.

MEZZALOGUE: *The Fulfillment of Nature*

1. *Ethics* 1106b.

2. *Ethics* 1105b–1106a.

3. *Ethics* 1106b.

4. My distinction between the "well-disposed" individual and the "well-controlled" individual corresponds to Aristotle's distinction between the *sophron* and the *enkrates*. This distinction is fundamental to the first two-thirds of Bk. VII of the *Ethics* (1145–52).

5. *Ethics* 1106a–7a.

6. Esp. *Ethics* 1115b–16a.

7. Esp. *Ethics* 1126b–27a.

8. "Justice is a sort of mean, not in the same way as the other virtues are, but in that it is realized in a median amount, while injustice belongs to the extremes." See *Ethics* 1133b–34a.

9. *Ethics* 1117b–28b.

10. Aristotle contrasts these "intellectual" excellences with the others he calls "moral." See *Ethics*, Bk. VI.

11. Plato accepts the fourfold classification of the excellences into courage, ease in self-command, wisdom, and justice for the purposes of his *Republic*, although not in other places. This is probably a strategic concession to the general opinion of his countrymen.

12. Which focus on the idea that we were not made for ourselves.

13. See his *Philosophical Investigations*.

14. The nature of this opportunity is a matter of dispute. Aristotle's suggestion that dramatic spectacle purges the audience of fear and pity seems to contradict Socrates' claim that it only whips them up. In the traditional interpretation, Aristotle is trying to show that, far from corroding character, the presentation of a tragedy can serve a moral function. Recent critics, though, have leaned toward the view that Aristotle only wants to show that the pleasures of tragedy are harmless. At least one critic even argues that Aristotle and Socrates were in essential agreement over the purgative action of tragedy; at least, this is how I read Bloom. Taken too literally, the idea of an emotional "purge" is probably misleading, for the soul is not like the bowels (or even like a tank or reservoir, as I argue against Freud and others in Chapter 5). We need, but lack, a theory of "consummatory" moral experience. The texts

for this note are the *Poetics* and *Politics* of Aristotle, and the *Republic* of Plato, including Bloom's commentary.

15. *After Virtue*, 175.

16. *Aristotle: Nicomachean Ethics VI*, 46–47.

17. *Reason and Human Good in Aristotle*, esp. 22.

18. *After Virtue*, 176.

19. Ibid., 175–76.

20. See ibid., 186–87ff.

21. See how he connects this with other issues in *Democracy in America*, Vol. II, Pt. II, Chs. 1–8.

22. Thomas says that "the proper effect of law is to lead its subjects to their proper virtue: and since virtue is *that which makes its subject good*, it follows that the proper effect of law is to make those to whom it is given, good, either simply or in some particular respect." This is from the *Treatise on Law* (in the *Summa Theologica*), Question 92, Article 1.

23. *Treatise on Law*, Question 96, Article 2, Reply to Objection 2. In the body of this article, Thomas argues that "laws imposed on men should . . . be in keeping with their condition."

24. Ibid., Article 3: "But law . . . is ordained to the common good. Wherefore there is no virtue whose acts cannot be prescribed by the law. Nevertheless human law does not prescribe concerning all the acts of every virtue: but only in regard to those that are ordainable to the common good."

25. Ibid., Article 2, Reply to Objection 2.

26. *Providence and Evil*.

CHAPTER FOUR: *Nature Writ Large*

1. Aristotle's *Ethics* ends in midthought with the remark that the topics under discussion lead directly into political science, "to which we now turn"—presumably in his *Politics*.

2. See the discussion of what Rawls calls "perfectionism" in his *Theory of Justice*, esp. 325–32. Unfortunately, Rawls distorts the idea by focusing on excellence in art, science, and "culture" rather than on excellence of character per se.

3. This can be found in *John Stuart Mill: Three Essays*. See Ch. 2, esp. 166–73.

4. *Theory of Justice*, 360.

5. This terminology is not meant to endorse the "systems" theory of David Easton, which I have criticized elsewhere.

6. *Considerations on Representative Government*, 171–73.

7. For social-choice theory, see, e.g., Kenneth Arrow, *Social Choice and Individual Values*; Amartya K. Sen, *Collective Choice and Social Welfare*; and, in a somewhat different vein, James Buchanan and Gordon Tullock, *The Calculus of Consent*. There are indications that some social-choice theorists may be ready to reconsider the outlook I am about to discuss (William Riker and Robert Axelrod spring to mind), but I do not discuss these possibilities here. For examples of the "neutralist" school of liberal ethics and related tendencies in jurisprudence, see Ronald Dworkin, "Liberalism"; Bruce A. Ackerman, *Social Justice in the Liberal State*; and John Hart Ely, *Democracy in Distrust*. Neutralist Ackerman borrows heavily from social-choice theory and explicitly compares the two approaches in a footnote on p. 11.

8. See Kenneth O. May, "A Set of Independent, Necessary, and Sufficient Conditions for Simple Majority Decision."

9. Thus Rawls on p. 192 of *A Theory of Justice*: "The virtues are sentiments . . . regulated by a higher-order desire, in this case a desire to act from the corresponding moral principles."

10. See his discussions of "reflective equilibrium" in *A Theory of Justice*, esp. 20–21, 48–51, 578–79.

11. *Ethics* 1098, in broad paraphrase.

12. This is "proportional" as contrasted with "arithmetic" equality, a concept used in both the *Ethics* and the *Politics*; see esp. *Politics* 1281.

13. See esp. *Politics* 1283.

14. *After Virtue*, esp. 152, 183.

15. Ibid., 204 and 207 respectively.

16. See his *Christianity Rediscovered*, 28–29.

17. The book is *De Officiis*, usually (and misleadingly) translated under the title "On Duty." For discussion of the sense of the term *officium*, see Harry G. Edinger's introductory essay in the Bobbs-Merrill edition of the work.

18. See his *Democracy in America*, esp. Vol. II, Pt. II, Ch. 2; and Vol. II, Pt. III, Ch. 13.

19. See esp. *Ethics* 1155; but friendship is the major topic of Book VIII, and Aristotle returns to the relation between friendship and justice in 1159–61.

20. This is from *Democracy in America*, Vol. II, Pt. II, Ch. 15 (p. 543 in the Doubleday edition, trans. George Lawrence).

21. See *Ethics*, the last few lines of 1123a, then 1123b–25a.

22. Nietzsche talked about this everywhere—in *Beyond Good and Evil*, *The Genealogy of Morals*, *Twilight of the Idols*, *The Antichrist*, and other places; see esp. his remarks on the "Laws of Manu" in *Twilight of the Idols*.

23. See esp. *Politics* 1253–55.

24. As Aristotle did; see his *Rhetoric*.

25. The distinction between act-, rule-, and institutional utilitarianism is also based on the level at which the fundamental principle is applied.

26. "Of Property."

27. Sometimes it is not done away with, but merely trivialized. For citations, see n. 10.

28. See esp. *On Liberty*, which can be found in *John Stuart Mill: Three Essays*.

29. The *idea* of the invisible hand pervades the latter work, although I find only a few uses of the phrase itself: e.g., in Pt. IV, Ch. I (p. 304 in the Liberty Classics edition), where character is not the topic.

30. His approval is implied by his use of the British regime as an example in the later chapters of the *Second Treatise*.

31. *Considerations on Representative Government*, 204–6.

32. The *question* whether virtue can be taught is attributed by Plato to Socrates; the *answer* I have given here belongs, by my interpretation, to Aristotle.

33. See esp. *Politics* 1252–53.

34. See esp. *Federalist #62, 63*.

35. The argument is found in *Politics* 1276–77.

36. This tension also pervades his essay *Utilitarianism*, where it is easy to see.

CHAPTER FIVE: *Nature Compromised*

1. In *The Prince*, Ch. XV, Machiavelli proclaims that "since my intention is to write something useful for anyone who understands it, it seemed more suitable to me to search after the effectual truth of the matter rather than its imagined one. And many writers have imagined for themselves republics and principalities that have never been seen nor known to exist in reality; for there is such a gap between how one lives and how one ought to live that anyone who abandons what is done for what ought to be done learns his ruin rather than his preservation: for a man who wishes to make a vocation of being good at all times will come to ruin among so many who are not good." Evidence of how widespread this sentiment became can be found in Albert O. Hirschman, *The Passions and the Interests*, 12–14.

2. This is from "Lord Bacon" in Milford's collection of *Literary Essays Contributed to the Edinburgh Review by Lord Macaulay*, 382–83.

3. Ibid., 387. Macaulay says he is speaking of Bacon, but he undeniably identifies with the subject of his character sketch.

4. See his *Republic*, esp. 462–64.

5. *Republic* 439e–41.

6. The next few page references are to the Liberty Classics edition of the work.

7. Smith, Pt. I, Sec. I, Ch. 1: "But whatever may be the cause of sympathy, or however it may be excited, nothing pleases us more than to observe in other men a fellow-feeling with all the emotions of our own breast" (p. 54). "Sympathy, however, enlivens joy and alleviates grief. It enlivens joy by presenting another source of satisfaction; and it alleviates grief by insinuating into the heart almost the only agreeable sensation which it is at that time capable of receiving" (p. 55).

8. Smith sometimes uses the term to denote the concordance itself, as in ibid., 49: "Pity and compassion are words appropriated to signify our fellow-feeling with the sorrow of others. Sympathy, though its meaning was, perhaps, originally the same, may now, however, without much impropriety, be made use of to denote our fellow-feeling with any passion whatever." However, this is atypical and slightly misleading.

9. This problem occupies Smith esp. in Pt. I, Sec. II.

10. Ibid., 71 (Pt. I, Sec. I, Ch. 5).

11. Ibid., 71–72.

12. Ibid., 80–81 (Pt. I, Sec. II, Ch. 1).

13. As Smith puts the matter in ibid., 208 (Pt. III, Ch. 2): "Man naturally desires, not only to be loved, but to be lovely; or to be that thing which is the natural and proper object of love. He naturally dreads, not only to be hated, but to be hateful; or to be that thing which is the natural and proper object of hatred. He desires not only praise, but praise-worthiness; or to be that thing which, though it should be praised by nobody, is, however, the natural and proper object of praise. He dreads, not only blame, but blame-worthiness; or to be that thing which, though it should be blamed by nobody, is, however, the natural and proper object of blame."

14. The dependence of the Impartial Spectator on prior experience with partial spectators is made especially clear in ibid., 204–5 (Pt. III, Ch. 1), where in a passage strongly evocative of Rousseau's "second" discourse, Smith says that an individual who grew up to manhood "in some solitary place, without any communication with his own species" could not possibly have any image of himself at all. The most important discussions of the Impartial Spectator are found in Pt. II, Sec. II, Ch. 2; and Pt. III, Chs. 1 and 2.

15. This is found in ibid., 206 (Pt. III, Ch. 1).

16. "The jurisdiction of the man without is founded altogether in the desire of actual praise, and in the aversion to actual blame. The jurisdiction of the man within is founded altogether in the desire of praiseworthiness, and in the aversion to blameworthiness" (ibid., 227, in Pt. III, Ch. 2). So Smith says; but his description of the psychodynamics suggests more the *converse* in both cases.

17. See esp. "The Ego and the Super-Ego (Ego Ideal)," which is the third chapter of *The Ego and the Id*; also Lecture XXXI of the *New Introductory Lectures on Psychoanalysis*, "The Dissection of the Psychical Personality."

18. This passage is found in *Eichmann in Jerusalem*, 150.

19. Subtitled *Political Arguments for Capitalism before Its Triumph*.

20. This is the title of the section covering pp. 20–31 of Hirschman's book.

21. *The Passions and the Interests*, 20.

22. Stimulus conflict and related matters are discussed in Hinde's *Animal Behavior*.

23. Namely Bk. V, Chs. 12–20. Page references in the following notes are to the Penguin edition.

24. This flaw in Hirschman's otherwise impeccable scholarship is probably due to his reliance upon a secondary work rather than Augustine's own text. The work is Herbert A. Deane's *Political and Social Ideas of St. Augustine* (New York: Columbia University Press, 1963), to which Hirschman refers in notes.

25. *City of God*, 199 (Bk. V, Ch. 12).

26. Ibid.

27. Ibid., 197.

28. Ibid., 199. The phrase "tricks of the canvasser" and the word "merit" are also Augustine's.

29. The "lust to accumulate wealth—that corrupter of morality" is attacked on p. 199. Ambition for glory is not distinguished from ambition for domination until Bk. V, Ch. 19 (ibid., 212–14).

30. This passage is from the first paragraph of Bk. V, Ch. 14 (ibid., 203). Fifteen pages later, in Ch. 20, Augustine also says that should the virtues become the "slaves of human glory," "Prudence would exercise no foresight, Justice make no dispensations, Fortitude show no endurance, Temperance impose no moderation, except so far as to win man's approval." Contrast Smith on sympathy.

31. For the sense of the term "love," see Bk. XIV, Ch. 7. See also Ch. 5 concerning the first fallacy, and concerning the second, Chs. 6, 8, 9. In Ch. 9 (ibid., 566), Augustine concludes: "It comes to this then:

NOTES TO CHAPTER 5

we must lead a right life to reach the goal of a life of felicity; and this right kind of life exhibits all those emotions in the right way, and a misdirected life in a misdirected way."

32. As well as *The Prince*, but the *Discourses* is a better source for this.

33. I am using the Bondanella-Musa translation, which is given, in part, in *The Portable Machiavelli*. These lines are from p. 233.

34. Lovers and philosophers in the *Symposium*, tyrants and philosophers in the *Republic*.

35. In Aristotle's case the prescription is buried in a distinction between three kinds of crimes: those that men commit to obtain necessities, those they commit in order to rid themselves of painful desires, and those they commit in order to obtain pleasure without pain. Concerning the third, he says: "Men may not only commit crime to cure a desire they already feel: they may start some desire just in order to enjoy the sort of pleasure which is unaccompanied by pain. What is the remedy? . . . we can only say that if there are men who want to get unmixed pleasure purely by their own independent effort, they will find no satisfaction except in the aid of philosophy; for all pleasures other than that of philosophy need the assistance of others." His very next words refer to tyranny: "The greatest crimes are committed not for the sake of necessities, but for the sake of superfluities. Men do not become tyrants in order to avoid exposure to cold." These passages are from *Politics*, 1267a, in the translation of Ernest Barker.

36. Aristotle was tutor to Alexander in his youth, as Plato was tutor to Dionysius in his young manhood. According to some stories, the sentiments of Dionysius shifted so radically that he sold Plato into slavery, from which his friends had to redeem him; according to others, Plato merely had to leave Syracuse on very short notice. Although Aristotle had better luck with Alexander, he was evidently unable to deter him from carrying out his ambition to conquer the world—if, indeed, he even tried; but one would have thought that he would try, because such a conquest would mean the end of the *polis*.

37. As Allan Bloom points out in the introduction to his own translation of *Emile*.

38. Socrates' partner in conversation is trying to prove that tyrants enjoy the happiest lives.

39. For instance the opportunity to suck on a dry water nipple is reinforcing for thirsty rats, and the opportunity to perform intromission without ejaculating is reinforcing for sexually aroused male monkeys. See Robert A. Hinde, *Animal Behavior*.

40. This statement is found in *Federalist* #51.

41. See his *Theory of Moral Sentiments*, Pt. I, Sec. III, Ch. 2: "Of the origin of Ambition, and of the distinction of Ranks."

42. As Madison argues in *Federalist #62*, "It will be of little avail to the people that the laws are made by men of their own choice if the laws be so voluminous that they cannot be read, or so incoherent that they cannot be understood. . . . Another effect of public instability is the unreasonable advantage it gives to the sagacious, the enterprising, and the moneyed few over the industrious and uninformed mass of the people. Every new regulation . . . presents a new harvest to those who watch the change, and can trace its consequences; a harvest, reared not by themselves, but by the toils and cares of the great body of their fellow-citizens."

43. This particular paraphrase for Aristotle's approach to the "polity" was suggested to me by lines that occur in another context altogether—in *Politics* 1337a—where he says that "the purpose of education, like that of art generally, is simply to imitate nature by making her deficiencies good."

44. Cf. Harry Jaffa's interpretation of the polity, found in his essay "Aristotle": "As each rival claimant moderates his claim, in the light of the awareness that it can be turned against him, the idea of a common good in which the rival claims are harmonized emerges. And the idea of the common good necessarily implies both a limitation upon the absolutized claims of each party—including that of virtue—and a priority of the claims of virtue." I admit that my emphasis on "battling pathologies" is more nearly reconstruction than it is interpretation.

45. For this and the following remarks on Locke, see his *Second Treatise of Government*, esp. Ch. XIX, "Of the Dissolution of Government."

46. See Plato's *Republic* 501a–c, 540e–41a. Cf. Rousseau's *Social Contract*, Bk. II, Ch. VII, "On the Legislator."

47. Socrates' admission is in Plato's *Republic* 591e–92b. Machiavelli's raillery is in *The Prince*, Ch. XV.

48. In *The Prince*, Ch. XVIII, Machiavelli says that the prince must be like the lion and the fox. Now the virtue of the lion is an impetuous courage drawn from strength, while the virtue of the fox is cunning prudence. Courage and prudence, it so happens, are *two* of the four virtues considered cardinal by the Romans whom Machiavelli so admired; but unlike the Romans themselves, Machiavelli so construes them as to exclude the other two: temperance and justice. Of course, this is an indirect argument. But the implication of *The Prince*, Chs. XV–XIX, is that it is better to appear just than to be just, and Ma-

chiavelli's opposition to temperate "middle ways" is strikingly put in *The Prince*, Ch. XXV, as well as *Discourses*, Pt. I, Ch. XXVI.

49. The Prince is like Achilles insofar as he is *taught* by Chiron, and like Chiron himself insofar as he *learns* from him. See *The Prince*, Ch. XVIII.

50. See *Discourses*, Pt. I, Ch. XXVI, where Machiavelli advises the new Prince to "make everything over anew": "that is, to establish new rulers with new names, new authority, and new men; to make the rich poor, and the poor rich. . . . Besides this, he should build new cities, destroy existing ones, move the inhabitants from one place to another; in short, leave nothing intact in that province, nor permit either rank, institution, form of government, or wealth in your city which is not recognized as coming from you."

51. This justification is found in the first sentences of *The Prince*, Ch. VI.

52. Nietzsche very clearly recognized the mythical character of Machiavelli's ideal; see *The Will to Power*, Sec. 304. For an instructive contrast, see Aristotle's discussion of the "man of surpassing excellence" in *Politics* 1283a–85a.

EPILOGUE: *Nature Questioned*

1. The tale of the cave takes up Bk. VII of Plato's *Republic*.
2. *Republic* 533a.
3. *Republic* 517c.
4. See Plato's *Phaedo* 60a.
5. He admits his neglect of his family in Plato's *Apology* 31b.
6. See the drunken speech of Alcibiades beginning in 212e.
7. His friends chided him for an error he made on the one occasion when he needed to know the proper procedure for a motion.
8. Crito complains about this in 45e of the Platonic dialogue that bears his name. Years later, when Aristotle was also condemned but at a time when he was away from the city, he refused to return for his execution, reportedly saying that Athens would not be permitted to sin a second time against philosophy.
9. This is a major theme of Plato's *Phaedo*.
10. In Canto XXXIII of the *Paradiso*, which is the third canticle of his *Divine Comedy*, he confesses:

> As one who sees in dreams and wakes to find
>   the emotional impression of his vision
>   still powerful while its parts fade from his mind,

just such am I, having lost nearly all
the vision itself, while in my heart I feel
the sweetness of it yet distill and fall.

(From *The Paradiso* by Dante Alighieri, translated by John Ciardi. Copyright © 1961, 1967, 1970 by John Ciardi. Reprinted by arrangement with New American Library, New York, New York, and by permission of John Ciardi.)

11. The following passage is from his *Pensées*, Sec. 692, in Trotter's translation.

12. For Nietzsche, see esp. the first and third essays of *The Genealogy of Morals*; for Freud, see esp. *Moses and Monotheism*; for James, see *The Varieties of Religious Experience*.

13. The phrase, "genealogy of morals," besides providing a title for one of Nietzsche's best-known works, also has a close cousin in the heading of Pt. 5 of *Beyond Good and Evil:* "Natural History of Morals."

14. *How One Philosophizes with a Hammer* is the subtitle of Nietzsche's *Twilight of the Idols*.

15. See *The Will to Power*, Preface (esp. Secs. 2 and 3), and all of Pt. I.

16. The "death of God" is announced most dramatically in *Thus Spoke Zarathustra*, Prologue, Sec. 2; see also Pt. II, the section entitled "On the Blessed Isles."

17. In his later works, esp. *Beyond Good and Evil*, Nietzsche returns time and again to the metaphor of the labyrinth and the bestial terror it harbors. Other parts of the Theseus myth also have a place in his figurative system, in particular, the girl Ariadne, who gave Theseus a ball of golden thread that unwound by itself to lead him through the maze to the Minotaur, and Dionyssus, the god who compelled Theseus to desert Ariadne on an island so that he could take her for his own. "Human, all too human" is a favorite phrase of Nietzsche's; it provides the title of one of his middle-period books.

18. Because (a) uncorrupted philosophers shun power; (b) philosophers who seek power are corrupt; (c) an uncorrupted philosopher in power could not exact obedience from an unphilosophical city; and (d) reigning kings who are able to exact obedience shun philosophy. See *Republic*.

19. *The Attainment of Happiness*, paragraph 58. I am using Muhsin Mahdi's translation, from Lerner and Mahdi, eds., *Medieval Political Philosophy*.

20. See *Beyond Good and Evil*, Pt. 5, Sec. 203. Cf. Plato's *Republic* 491a–93a, in which Socrates expresses the same fears about philosophers.

21. See *Thus Spoke Zarathustra*, P. II, the section entitled "On Self-Overcoming." Chronologically this preceded *Beyond Good and Evil*, but the fears expressed in the latter work did not move Nietzsche to retract this slogan. In the overall context of the work he completed before his descent into madness, I think it is fair to regard this as his last word.

Bibliography

Ackerman, Bruce. *Social Justice in the Liberal State*. New Haven, Conn.: Yale University Press, 1980.

Alper, Joseph S. "Biological Determinism." *Telos* 31–34 (1977–78): 164–72.

Aquinas, Thomas. *Commentary on Aristotle's Physics*. Trans. Richard J. Blackwell, Richard J. Spath, and W. Edmund Thirlkel. New Haven, Conn.: Yale University Press, 1963.

——. *Summa Theologica*. Trans. Fathers of the English Dominican Province. Westminister, Md.: Christian Classics, 1981.

Arendt, Hannah. *Eichmann in Jerusalem: A Report on the Banality of Evil*. New York: Viking Press, 1964.

——. *The Human Condition: A Study of the Central Dilemmas Facing Modern Man*. New York: Doubleday, 1959.

Aristophanes. *The Clouds*. Trans. William Arrowsmith. New York: New American Library, 1962.

Aristotle. *Nichomachean Ethics*. Trans. Martin Ostwald. Indianapolis, Ind.: Bobbs-Merrill, 1962.

——. *Politics*. Trans. Ernest Barker. New York: Oxford University Press, 1946.

Arrow, Kenneth. *Social Choice and Individual Values*. 2d ed. New Haven, Conn.: Yale University Press, 1963.

Augustine of Hippo. *The City of God*. Trans. Henry Betenson, ed. David Knowles. New York: Penguin Books, 1972.

Bacon, Francis. *New Organon and Related Writings*. Ed. Fulton H. Anderson. Indianapolis, Ind.: Bobbs-Merrill, 1960.

Barash, David P. *Sociobiology and Behavior*. New York: Elsevier, 1977.

Barlow, George W. Review of Wilson's *Sociobiology*. *Animal Behavior* 24 (1976): 700–701. See Wilson, Edward O.

BIBLIOGRAPHY

Bentham, Jeremy. *An Introduction to the Principles of Morals and Legislation.* Ed. Laurence J. Lafleur. New York: Hafner Press, 1948.

Bonner, John Tyler. *The Evolution of Culture in Animals.* Princeton, N.J.: Princeton University Press, 1980.

Brown, Norman O. *Love's Body.* New York: Vintage, 1966.

Buchanan, James, and Gordon Tullock. *The Calculus of Consent.* Ann Arbor: University of Michigan Press, 1962.

Burhoe, Ralph Wendell. "The Source of Civilization in the Natural Selection of Coadapted Information in Genes and Culture." *Zygon* 2 (1976): 263–303.

Campbell, Donald T. "On the Conflicts between Biological and Social Evolution and between Psychology and Moral Tradition." *American Psychologist* 30 (1975): 1103–26. For replies, see Wispe, Lauren G.

Chapman, John. See Pennock, Roland.

Cicero, Marcus Tullius. *De Officiis: On Duties.* Trans. Harry G. Edinger. Indianapolis, Ind.: Bobbs-Merrill, 1974.

Cloak, P. T., Jr. "Is a Cultural Ethology Possible?" *Human Ecology* 3 (1975): 161–82.

Cooper, John M. *Reason and Human Good in Aristotle.* Cambridge, Mass.: Harvard University Press, 1975.

Cropsey, Joseph, and Leo Strauss, eds. *History of Political Philosophy.* 2d ed. Chicago: University of Chicago Press, 1981.

Culler, Jonathan. *On Deconstruction: Theory and Criticism after Structuralism.* Ithaca, N.Y.: Cornell University Press, 1983. For a review, see Searle, John.

Dante Alighieri. *The Divine Comedy.* Trans. John Ciardi. New York: New American Library, 1961.

Dawkins, Richard. *The Selfish Gene.* London: Oxford University Press, 1976. For a reaction, see Lewontin, R. C.

Devore, Irwin. "The Evolution of Human Society." In J. F. Eisenberg and Wilton S. Dillon, eds., *Man and Beast: Comparative Social Behavior.* Washington, D.C.: Smithsonian Institution Press, 1971.

Dilthey, Wilhelm. "The Rise of Hermeneutics," an excerpt from *Die Entstehung der Hermeneutik.* In Paul Connerton, ed., *Critical Sociology.* New York: Penguin Books, 1976.

Dobzhansky, Theodosius. *Mankind Evolving: The Evolution of the Human Species.* New Haven, Conn.: Yale University Press, 1962.

Donovan, Vincent J. *Christianity Rediscovered.* 2d ed. Maryknoll, N.Y.: Orbis Books, 1982.

Dworkin, Ronald. "Liberalism." In Stuart Hampshire, ed., *Public and Private Morality.* Cambridge, Eng.: Cambridge University Press, 1978.

Easton, David. *A Framework for Political Analysis.* Englewood Cliffs, N.J.: Prentice-Hall, 1965.

Eckland, Bruce. "Darwin Rides Again." *American Journal of Sociology* 82 (1977): 692–97.

Eibl-Eibesfeldt, Irenäus. "Human Ethology: Concepts and Implications for the Sciences of Man." *Behavioral and Brain Sciences* 2 (1979): 1–57.

Ely, John Hart. *Democracy in Distrust.* Cambridge, Mass.: Harvard University Press, 1980.

"Encounter: Marvin Harris and E. O. Wilson Debate the Claims of Sociobiology." *Sciences* 18 (1978): 10–15, 27–28 (interviewer not named).

Federalist. See Rossiter, Clinton.

Fishkin, James S. *Beyond Subjective Morality: Ethical Reasoning and Political Philosophy.* New Haven, Conn.: Yale University Press, 1984.

——. "Liberal Theory and the Problem of Justification." Mimeograph. Prepared for the meetings of the American Society for Legal and Political Philosophy, December 1983, Boston, Mass.

Fleising, Usher. See Fox, Robin.

Foucault, Michel. *The Order of Things.* New York: Pantheon Books, 1970.

Fox, Robin, and Usher Fleising. "Human Ethology." *Annual Review of Anthropology* 5 (1976): 265–88.

Freud, Sigmund. *The Ego and the Id.* Trans. Joan Rivere, ed. James Strachey. New York: Norton, 1960.

——. *Moses and Monotheism.* Trans. Katherine Jones. New York: Vintage Books, 1939.

——. *New Introductory Lectures on Psychoanalysis.* Trans. James Strachey. New York: Norton, 1965.

Friedman, Milton. "The Methodology of Positive Economics." In W. Breit and H. M. Hochman, eds., *Readings in Microeconomics.* 2d ed. New York: Holt, Rinehart, & Winston, 1971.

Gadamer, Hans-Georg. "The Historicity of Understanding," an excerpt from *Truth and Method.* In Paul Connerton, ed., *Critical Sociology.* New York: Penguin Books, 1976.

Geach, P. T. *Providence and Evil.* Cambridge, Eng.: Cambridge University Press, 1977.

Geertz, Clifford. *The Interpretation of Cultures.* New York: Basic Books, 1973.

Gewirth, Alan. *Reason and Morality.* Chicago: University of Chicago Press, 1978.

——. "Rights and Virtues." *Review of Metaphysics* 38 (1985): 739–62.

Goffman, Erving. *The Presentation of Self in Everyday Life*. Garden City, N.Y.: Doubleday, 1959.

Greenwood, L. H. G. *Aristotle: Nicomachean Ethics VI*. Cambridge, Eng.: Cambridge University Press, 1909.

Griffin, Donald R. *The Question of Animal Awareness: Evolutionary Continuity of Mental Experience*. New York: Rockefeller University Press, 1976.

Hamilton, Alexander. See Rossiter, Clinton.

Hamilton, W. D. "Altruism and Related Phenomena, Mainly in Social Insects." *Annual Review of Ecological Systems* 3 (1972): 193–232.

———. "The Genetical Evolution of Social Behavior," pts. I, II. *Journal of Theoretical Biology* 7 (1964): 1–52.

Hare, R. M. *Freedom and Reason*. Oxford: Oxford University Press, 1963.

Harris, Marvin. See Encounter.

Hegel, G. W. F. *Hegel's Philosophy of Right*. Trans. T. M. Knox. New York: Oxford University Press, 1967.

———. *Phenomenology of Spirit*. Trans. A. V. Miller. New York: Oxford University Press, 1977.

Hinde, Robert A. *Animal Behavior: A Synthesis of Ethology and Comparative Psychology*. New York: McGraw-Hill, 1970.

Hirschman, Albert O. *The Passions and the Interests: Political Arguments for Capitalism before Its Triumph*. Princeton, N.J.: Princeton University Press, 1977.

Hobbes, Thomas. *Leviathan*. Ed. C. B. MacPherson. New York: Penguin Books, 1968.

Hume, David. *Hume's Moral and Political Philosophy*. Ed. Henry D. Aiken. New York: Hafner, 1948.

Jaffa, Harry. "Aristotle." In Joseph Cropsey and Leo Strauss, eds., *History of Political Philosophy*. 2d ed. Chicago: University of Chicago Press, 1981.

James, William. *The Varieties of Religious Experience*. Gifford Lectures, delivered at Edinburgh, 1901–2. New York: Modern Library, 1929.

Jay, John. See Rossiter, Clinton.

Kant, Immanuel. *Critique of Practical Reason*. Trans. Lewis White Beck. Indianapolis, Ind.: Bobbs-Merrill, 1956.

———. *Groundwork of the Metaphysics of Morals*. Trans. J. J. Paton. New York: Harper & Row, 1964.

Kojève, Alexandre. *Introduction to the Reading of Hegel*. Trans. James H. Nichols, Jr., ed. Allan Bloom. New York: Basic Books, 1969.

Krebs, John, and Robert M. May. "Social Insects and the Evolution of Altruism." *Nature* 260 (1976): 9–10.

Layzer, David. "On the Evolution of Intelligence and Social Behavior." In Ashley Montagu, ed., *Sociobiology Examined*. New York: Oxford University Press, 1980.

Lehrman, Daniel S. "A Critique of Konrad Lorentz's Theory of Instinctive Behavior." *Quarterly Journal of Biology* 28 (1953): 337–63.

Lerner, Ralph, and Muhsin Mahdi, eds. *Medieval Political Philosophy*. Ithaca, N.Y.: Cornell University Press, 1963.

Lévi-Strauss, Claude. *Structural Anthropology*. New York: Basic Books, 1963.

Lewis, C. S. *The Case for Christianity*. New York: Macmillan, 1943.

Lewontin, R. C. "Caricature of Darwinism." *Nature* 266 (1977): 283–84. See Dawkins, Richard.

——. "Evolution and the Theory of Games." *Journal of Theoretical Biology* 1 (1961): 382–403.

Locke, John. *An Essay Concerning Human Understanding*. Ed. Alexander Campbell Fraser. New York: Dover, 1959.

——. *Second Treatise of Government*. Ed. Thomas Peardon. Indianapolis, Ind.: Bobbs-Merrill, 1952.

Lorenz, Konrad. *Evolution and the Modification of Behavior*. Chicago: University of Chicago Press, 1965. See Lehrman, Daniel S.

——. *On Aggression*. New York: Harcourt, Brace & World, 1966.

Lumsden, Charles J. See Wilson, Edward O.

Macaulay, T. B. See Milford, Humphrey.

Machiavelli, Niccolo. *Discourses on the First Ten Books of Titus Livius*. Contained in part in Peter Bondanella and Mark Musa, trans., *The Portable Machiavelli*. New York: Penguin Books, 1979.

——. *The Prince*. In Peter Bandanella and Mark Musa, trans., *The Portable Machiavelli*. New York: Penguin Books, 1979.

MacIntyre, Alasdair. *After Virtue*. Notre Dame, Ind.: University of Notre Dame Press, 1981.

Madison, James. See Rossiter, Clinton.

Marx, Karl. "Alienated Labor." In Eugene Kamenka, ed., *The Portable Karl Marx*. New York: Penguin Books, 1983.

——. *Capital*. New York: International Publishers, 1967.

May, Kenneth O. "A Set of Independent, Necessary, and Sufficient Conditions for Simple Majority Decision." *Econometrica* 20 (1952).

May, Robert M. "Population Genetics and Cultural Inheritance." *Nature* 268 (1977): 11–13. See also Krebs, John.

Mayr, Ernst. "Behavior Programs and Evolutionary Strategies." *American Scientist* 62 (1974): 650–59.

Milford, Humphrey, ed. *Literary Essays Contributed to the Edinburgh Review by Lord Macaulay*. London: Oxford University Press, 1923.

Mill, J. S. *John Stuart Mill: Three Essays*. Ed. Richard Wollheim. Oxford: Oxford University Press, 1975.

Minsky, Marvin. "K-lines: A Theory of Memory." *Cognitive Science* 4 (1980): 117–33.

Moe, Terry. "On the Scientific Status of Rational Models." *American Journal of Political Science* 23 (1979): 215–43.

Montagu, Ashley. "On Instincts Again." *Current Anthropology* 17 (1976): 345–46. For a reply, see Vine, Ian.

——, ed. *Sociobiology Examined.* New York: Oxford University Press, 1980.

Moore, G. E. *Principia Ethica.* Cambridge, Eng.: Cambridge University Press, 1903.

Morgenstern, O. See Neumann, J. von.

Neumann, J. von, and O. Morgenstern. *Theory of Games and Economic Behavior.* Princeton, N.J.: Princeton University Press, 1947.

Nietzsche, Friedrich. *Beyond Good and Evil.* In Walter Kaufmann, trans., *Basic Writings of Nietzsche.* New York: Modern Library, 1968.

——. *The Gay Science.* Trans. Walter Kaufmann. New York: Random House, 1974.

——. *The Genealogy of Morals.* In Walter Kaufmann, trans., *Basic Writings of Nietzsche.* New York: Modern Library, 1968.

——. *On the Advantage and Disadvantage of History for Life.* Trans. Peter Preuss. Indianapolis, Ind.: Hackett, 1980.

——. *Thus Spoke Zarathustra.* In Walter Kaufmann, trans., *The Portable Nietzsche.* New York: Penguin Books, 1977.

——. *The Will to Power.* Trans. Walter Kaufmann and R. J. Hollingdale. New York: Random House, 1967.

Nozick, Robert. *Anarchy, State, and Utopia.* New York: Basic Books, 1974.

Parker, G. A. "Selfish Genes, Evolutionary Games, and the Adaptiveness of Behavior." *Nature* 274 (1978): 849–55.

Pascal, Blaise. *Pascal's Pensées.* Trans. W. F. Trotter. New York: Dutton, 1958.

Pennock, Roland, and John Chapman, eds. *NOMOS XVII: Human Nature and Politics.* New York: Lieber-Atherton, 1976.

Petryszak, Nicholas. "The Biosociology of the Social Self." *Sociological Quarterly* 20 (1979): 291–303.

Plato. *The Collected Dialogues, Including the Letters.* Ed. Edith Hamilton and Huntington Cairns. Princeton, N.J.: Princeton University Press, 1961.

——. *The Republic of Plato.* Trans. Allan Bloom. New York: Basic Books, 1968.

Pocock, J. G. A. "Custom and Grace, Form and Matter: An Approach to Machiavelli's Concept of Innovation." In M. Fleisher, ed., *Machiavelli and the Nature of Political Thought.* New York: Atheneum, 1972. For a reply, see Polka, Brayton.

Polka, Brayton. "Commentary." In M. Fleisher, ed., *Machiavelli and the Nature of Political Thought*. New York: Atheneum, 1972. See Pocock, J. G. A.

Price, G. R. See Smith, J. Maynard.

Pugh, George Edgin. *The Biological Origin of Human Values*. New York: Basic Books, 1977.

Rae, Douglas, Douglas Yates, Jennifer Hochschild, Joseph Morone, and Carol Fessler. *Equalities*. Cambridge, Mass.: Harvard University Press, 1981.

Rawls, John. *A Theory of Justice*. Cambridge, Mass.: Harvard University Press, 1971.

Rorty, Amelie Oksenberg, ed. *Explaining Emotions*. Berkeley: University of California Press, 1980.

Rossiter, Clinton, ed. *The Federalist Papers*. New York: New American Library, 1961.

Rousseau, Jean-Jacques. *Emile; Or, On Education*. Trans. Allan Bloom. New York: Basic Books, 1979.

———. *The First and Second Discourses*. Trans. and ed. Roger and Judith Masters. New York: St. Martin's Press, 1964.

———. *On the Social Contract*. Trans. and ed. Roger and Judith Masters. New York: St. Martin's Press, 1978.

Searle, John. "The Word Turned Upside Down." *New York Review of Books*, October 1983, 74–79. See Culler, Jonathan.

Sen, Amartya K. *Collective Choice and Social Welfare*. San Francisco: Holden-Day, 1970.

Simpson, George Gaylord. "The Biological Nature of Man." *Science* 156 (1966): 472–78.

Smith, Adam. *The Theory of Moral Sentiments*. Indianapolis, Ind.: Liberty Classics, 1976.

Smith, J. Maynard. "The Ecology of Sex." In J. R. Krebs and N. B. Davies, eds., *Behavioral Ecology: An Evolutionary Approach*. Oxford: Blackwell Scientific, 1978.

———. "Evolution and the Theory of Games." *American Scientist* 64 (1976): 41–45.

———. "The Theory of Games and the Evolution of Animal Conflicts." *Journal of Theoretical Biology* 47 (1974): 209–21.

Smith, J. Maynard, and G. R. Price. "The Logic of Animal Conflict." *Nature* 246 (1973): 15–18.

Smith, Steven. *Reading Althusser*. Ithaca, N.Y.: Cornell University Press, 1984.

Strauss, Leo. *Natural Right and History*. Chicago: University of Chicago Press, 1953. See also Cropsey, Joseph.

Thompson, James N. See Wispe, Lauren G.

Tinbergen, Nikolaas. *The Study of Instinct*. Oxford: Clarendon Press, 1958.

Tiryakian, Edward A. "Biosocial Man, *Sic et Non*." *American Journal of Sociology* 82 (1976): 701–6.

Tocqueville, Alexis de. *Democracy in America*. Trans. George Lawrence, ed. J. P. Mayer. New York: Doubleday, 1969.

Trivers, Robert L. "The Evolution of Reciprocal Altruism." *Quarterly Review of Biology* 46 (1971): 35–57.

Tullock, Gordon. See Buchanan, James.

Vine, Ian. "Reply." *Current Anthropology* 17 (1976): 346–47. See Montague, Ashley.

Wade, Nicholas. "Sociobiology: Troubled Birth for New Discipline." *Science* 191 (1976): 1151–55.

Weber, Max. "Science as a Vocation." In H. H. Gerth and C. Wright Mills, trans., *From Max Weber: Essays in Sociology*. New York: Oxford University Press, 1958.

——. "Value judgment in Social Science." In W. G. Runciman, ed., and E. Matthews, trans., *Max Weber: Selections in Translation*. New York: Cambridge University Press, 1978.

Williams, Charles. *The Figure of Beatrice*. New York: Noonday, 1961.

Wilson, Edward O. "Biology and the Social Sciences." *Daedalus* 106 (1977): 127–40.

——. *The Insect Societies*. Cambridge, Mass.: Harvard University Press, 1971.

——. *On Human Nature*. Cambridge, Mass.: Harvard University Press, 1978.

——. "Sociobiology: A New Approach to Understanding the Basis of Human Nature." *New Scientist* 69 (1976): 342–48.

——. *Sociobiology: The New Synthesis*. Cambridge, Mass.: Harvard Univeristy Press, 1975. For a review, see Barlow, George W.; see also Encounter.

Wilson, Edward O., and Charles J. Lumsden. *Genes, Mind, and Culture: The Coevolutionary Process*. Cambridge, Mass.: Harvard University Press, 1981.

Winch, Peter. *The Idea of a Social Science and Its Relation to Philosophy*. New York: Humanities Press, 1958.

Wispe, Lauren G., James N. Thompson, Jr., et al. "The War between the Words: Biological versus Social Evolution and Some Related Issues." Includes a reprise by Donald T. Campbell. *American Psychologist* 31 (1976): 341–84. See Campbell, Donald T.

Wittgenstein, Ludwig. *Philosophical Investigations*. Trans. G. E. M. Anscombe. New York: Macmillan, 1970.

Index

Library of Congress Cataloging-in-Publication Data

Budziszewski, J., 1952–
 The resurrection of nature.

 Bibliography: p.
 Includes index.
 1. Political ethics. 2. Natural law. I. Title.
JA79.B83 1986   172   86-6283
ISBN 0-8014-1900-X